Pastor Walter Hallam is o₁   to do great and mighty things for the kingdom of God in these last days. His powerful delivery of God's Word and his sensitivity to what the Holy Spirit is saying to the church today is causing multitudes of people to experience a fresh and new relationship with the Lord Jesus Christ. I strongly encourage every Christian to read Pastor Hallam's newest book, *From This Day On . . .*, and get ready to enter into a new dimension of victorious living.

—JERRY SAVELLE
JERRY SAVELLE MINISTRIES
CROWLEY, TEXAS

I'd like to introduce you to Pastor Walter Hallam. As an evangelist I have had the honor of ministering in many different churches across the U.S. and abroad. I've met many great men of God and can say with all honesty that I believe Brother Hallam to be one of God's best! Although I have ministered at his church many times, I find that *I'm* the one who leaves having been ministered to! He is a unique and gracious man of God who I believe understands the fullness of the fivefold ministry in a way that few men do. I think he is a strong and honest teacher of the Word who flows greatly in the gifts of the Spirit. I know you're going to be blessed by what he has to say in this book. So get ready to take off the limits and break out of the old mold. Brother Hallam's going to show you how to get past the past and enjoy true freedom in Jesus *From This Day On!*

—JESSE DUPLANTIS
JESSE DUPLANTIS MINISTRIES
NEW ORLEANS, LOUISIANA

FROM THIS DAY ON . . .

FROM THIS DAY ON . . .

WALTER

Hallam

FROM THIS DAY ON . . . by Walter Hallam
Published by Creation House
A part of Strang Communications Company
600 Rinehart Road
Lake Mary, Florida 32746
www.creationhouse.com

Unless otherwise noted, all Scripture quotations are from the New King James Version of the Bible. Copyright © 1979, 1980, 1982 by Thomas Nelson, Inc., publishers. Used by permission.

Scripture quotation marked KJV are from the King James Version of the Bible.

Scripture quotations marked NAS are from the New American Standard Bible. Copyright © 1960, 1962, 1963, 1968, 1971, 1972, 1973, 1975, 1977 by the Lockman Foundation. Used by permission. (www.lockman.org)

Scripture quotation marked NIV are from the Holy Bible, New International Version. Copyright © 1973, 1978, 1984, International Bible Society. Used by permission.

Library of Congress Catalog Card Number: 00-102010
International Standard Book Number: 0-88419-691-7

0 1 2 3 4 5 6 7 VERSA 8 7 6 5 4 3 2 1
Printed in the United States of America

This book is dedicated to Cindy, my beautiful wife of twenty-four years. When we first married, we had very little vision for ourselves except to endeavor to serve God together and remain in love with each other all of our lives. Then I found out those two qualities are the greatest vision any man and woman can have.

To realize your dreams, to serve the Lord and to love your wife all your life requires two people. Cindy has always been my dearest friend and companion, and she makes it so easy to stay in love with her. Her desire to be a virtuous woman, mother, wife and Christian companion is the main reason we have come this far.

She now speaks publicly and ministers many times a week and still finds time to be a mother to our three teenagers and an anointed wife to me. I am sure we will finish our calling together, *from this day on.*

Contents

Foreword

IN MARCH 2000, during my ministry with Pastor Walter Hallam and the four thousand people jamming his church, he had just begun to get the full revelation from God for this book. He shared with me the powerful word of Psalm 40 where David was being held back by the *echoes* of his past. David felt as if he were in a horrible pit, sinking deeper into miry clay. With the noise flooding his ears and mind with the echoes of bad events in the past, David finally realized he couldn't live in the "echo chamber" any longer—all the noise was blocking out his opportunity to hear the voice of God to bring him up and out into a new beginning. In Psalm 40:1, David says, "I waited patiently for the LORD...and He heard my cry."

Just as David did, I too get caught up in my spirit from dwelling on the mistakes of my past.

As Walter continued sharing, I "caught" where he was leading. "Walter," I said, "write this in a book as quickly as you can."

He replied, "You really think it will free up a lot of people from a past that is clinging to them, numbing them from hearing God's voice and seeing the future of glory God has for them?"

"Yes, I do," I answered.

"Then I'll do it," he said.

When I began to read the manuscript, I found the Spirit of God using my dear friend Walter Hallam to speak to me, revealing things in my past onto which I'd been unconsciously holding. But He didn't stop there. He showed me exactly how to come out of the miry clay and to hear a new song in my heart announcing that my future is as bright as the promises of God.

I am very careful about the books for which I will write a foreword. I have to feel it, taste it and see things in it from God for me before I can encourage others to know it is a worthy book, one they can't lay down until they've read every word—and then read it again. My life has been "lifted" out of some bad echo chambers of the past, and I'm convinced that Walter's anointed, stirring word pictures straight out of the Bible and life as most of us have lived it will do the same for you.

I believe as you read and absorb *From This Day On . . .* , written by a man of God who is one of the most gifted writers I know, you will say, "Thank You, God. *From this day on* are going to be my best days ahead."

God bless you as you read this book.

—ORAL ROBERTS, FOUNDER/CHANCELLOR
ORAL ROBERTS UNIVERSITY

PART
One

Echoes of the Mind

Do YOU KNOW someone who lives in an echo chamber? Whose life seems to be controlled by thoughts from the past? Who can't seem to get beyond lingering echoes from past problems? A person for whom today never dawns, but yesterday rules with an iron scepter from sunup to sundown?

Do you ever find *yourself* living in an echo chamber?

What is an echo? It is the residual sound from an actual happening. When I think of echoes I think of times I have sat on the edge of a cliff facing a big mountain range. When I yelled or clapped my hands, after a few seconds the sound came right back to me, then reverberated down the canyon. I think of times I have been in a gymnasium watching a basketball game in its final seconds. The noise level rose, and the screams and yells of the crowd bounced off the walls, echoing back and forth until I felt I had lost half my hearing. Or I think of times I have driven in the car with someone who turned up the music so loud that the echoes ricocheted off the

1

windows and swirled around me until I thought I couldn't concentrate on the road anymore.

If you've had one of these experiences, then you know what it's like to live in an echo chamber.

> *What is an echo? It is the residual sound from an actual happening.*

An echo chamber is a room where your voice bounces back at you, where every noise is multiplied and repeated over and over again. I have been a pastor for fifteen years. After having counseled hundreds of people in my own flock and ministering worldwide in dozens of countries, I have discovered that many Christians are living in their own, personalized echo chambers. These echo chambers are places where thoughts from occurrences from the past live on as though they still were real. Things that have already happened—things forgiven, dead and gone—take on a second life and rise to a position of control in a person's life. The voice of God is lost in the lives of those who are trying to live on an echo. And it is killing these people—spiritually and physically.

Once a lady introduced herself to me in the foyer of my church and said, "Hi, my name is So-and-so, and you should know that I was abused sexually as a child." This woman was in her fifties, and the person who had abused her had been dead for many years. Sexual abuse can be devastating, but this woman was voluntarily living in an echo chamber. She needed help to learn to wake up every morning and say, "This is the day that the Lord has made; I will rejoice and be glad in it," instead of saying, "I was abused as a child."

She was stuck in an echo.

Stuck in the Past

Thousands, maybe millions, of people live the same way, refusing to stand up to the echoes of the past that haunt them. They say, "I am an alcoholic." "My mother didn't tell me she loved me." "I grew up poor." "My father died when I was young." Instead of experiencing the renewed mercies of the Lord every morning, they run around the same track like a delusioned athlete headed toward certain defeat.

During the day, everything they see, learn or think about is filtered through that thought. When they go to sleep, they tell themselves the same thing. Every day becomes a stage where the echoes of the past put on a masquerade of real living.

Does this sound like your life? Have you heard the echoes to which I'm referring? Some people—perhaps you—have lived with echoes virtually from the time they were born. Perhaps while you were a young child someone told you that you were ugly, no good or that you would never amount to much. From that moment until now you've had that echo bouncing around in your mind like echoes in the Grand Canyon. You have thought about the issue more times than you can count. Instead of understanding that you are gloriously and wondrously made—as the Psalms say—you are listening to your echoes:

- I'm not good enough.
- I'm not rich enough.
- I don't have the perfect body.
- I'm not a very good mother.
- I'm a poor excuse for a man.

Do any of these echoes sound familiar? If so, you are not alone. You would be amazed how many people have strong hurts in their past and wake up every morning in the echo chamber.

As the Holy Spirit began to talk to me one day, He gave me one of the greatest revelations I have ever had. He told me that *a thought is nothing more than an echo in your mind, a thought about something from your yesterday that no longer exists except in the mind.* An echo is the residual product of something that was real, but is no longer real. It's a sound that is gone!

Yet for many, these echoes are in the driver's seat of life. Every time you go to Wal-Mart or a restaurant or the mall you are surrounded by people who are living in the past, who are hearing echoes every minute of the day. They may look like normal people, but inside they have conceded defeat. Even if they don't live daily in the echo chamber, at least they believe that someday the echoes will return. They live in a constant state of expectation that the past will continue to haunt them. They've been hurt. They've been lied to. They're in what the Bible calls *a horrible pit* (Ps. 40:2).

Fear Is Faith in Reverse

The greatest day in your life is when you recognize that you have begin living in an echo chamber, and you begin saying *no* to the echoes and *yes* to the voice of the Lord. That will be the day you find your destiny.

Consider King David for a moment. He portrays for us a picture of a man stuck in an echo chamber. He had sinned, failed, missed God and lived through it. He had been involved in adultery and murder. Under the Law there was no repentance or sacrifice for the sins he had committed. The Law's answer to murder and adultery was to have the offender stoned or killed. David was a man after God's own heart, but not always a man after God's own actions.

In Psalm 40, David expressed his heart-wrenching desire for a powerful move of God to deliver him from the effects and memories of his past. But David waited patiently for the Lord. He needed personal revival. He was in a time of torment, yet he found it in himself to wait on God. Waiting takes more faith than we may realize. To wait on God is to believe that He has heard us and will respond. David said, "I waited patiently for the LORD; and He inclined to me, and heard my cry" (v. 1).

The devil will tell us that God doesn't hear our cries. I'm sure we all have experienced that particular doubt, but it is nothing more than a trick to erode our faith. Don't give in! The next time the devil tells you that God doesn't hear your cry, find your strength in the Word of God.

> But know that the LORD has set apart for Himself him who is godly; the LORD will hear when I call to Him.
>
> —PSALM 4:3

> He shall call upon Me, and I will answer him; I will be with him in trouble; I will deliver him and honor him.
>
> —PSALM 91:15

> It shall come to pass that before they call, I will answer; and while they are still speaking, I will hear.
>
> —ISAIAH 65:24

> Call to Me, and I will answer you, and show you great and mighty things, which you do not know.
>
> —JEREMIAH 33:3

> I am the good shepherd; and I know My sheep, and am known by My own.
>
> —JOHN 10:14

David was at a critical time in his life when God wanted to renew his mind for the purposes that were to come. He was dealing with thoughts of his sin, his guilt and his fears. He was a man after God's own heart, but he still didn't have a renewed mind. I imagine he woke up every day thinking about his failures.

In Psalm 40:2 David said that God delivered him from a "horrible pit." "Horrible pit" can also be translated "room of noise." I was meditating on this one day, and the Lord said to me, "A room of noise is an echo chamber." David had a choice just as we have a choice. Would he continue to listen to the echoes of his past? Would he let them steal his days and nights, steal his destiny, steal his dreams? Would he become irrelevant to the purposes of God in the generation God was establishing? Or would he wait in faith with his ear tuned to the voice of the Lord? Would he reject those echoes as nothing more than residual traces of a former reality?

Reputation Is an Echo, but Revelation Is a Voice

Essentially David was saying, "I am in an echo chamber; my life is going in slow motion, and I'm stuck in miry clay"—just like the lives of many Christians today. Some of us are walking knee deep in sand when we ought to be sprinting on solid ground. But David said, "[God] also brought me up out of a horrible pit, out of the miry clay, and set my feet upon a rock" (Ps. 40:2). Who is the rock? He is Christ, the Rock of revelation.

David learned what we must also learn: *Reputation is an echo, but revelation is a reality.* Our reputation is based on what we did in the past, but God speaks new revelation into our lives to define our future. He removes us from the echo chamber and sets our feet on Christ, the Rock of revelation.

Christ's revelation frees us from the past, and we are

empowered to take dominion over our thoughts. That's why in all thirteen of Paul's epistles he told his readers to renew their minds, to take control of their thoughts.

Let's look at some of Paul's instructions:

> Be not conformed to this world: but be ye transformed by the renewing of your mind.
>
> —ROMANS 12:2, KJV

> Casting down imaginations, and every high thing that exalteth itself against the knowledge of God, and bringing into captivity every thought to the obedience of Christ.
>
> —2 CORINTHIANS 10:5, KJV

> Be renewed in the spirit of your mind.
>
> —EPHESIANS 4:23, KJV

> Let this mind be in you, which was also in Christ Jesus.
>
> —PHILIPPIANS 2:5, KJV

> For this cause we also, since the day we heard it, do not cease to pray for you, and to desire that ye might be filled with the knowledge of his will in all wisdom and spiritual understanding.
>
> —COLOSSIANS 1:9, KJV

> Now we beseech you, brethren, by the coming of our Lord Jesus Christ…that ye be not soon shaken in mind, or be troubled.
>
> —2 THESSALONIANS 2:1–2, KJV

The Word of God says, "When I was a child…I thought as a child: but when I became a man, I put away childish things" (1 Cor. 13:11, KJV). This means to put off thoughts that occupied us in the past: childish failures, childish disappointments, childish echoes—anything that would detract from our whole and healthy life in Christ today or keep us from moving forward into His purpose for our lives.

God commands us to take control of thoughts, cast down imaginations and pull down strongholds, which are past hurts, religious dogmas, thoughts and cultural traditions that defy Jesus and hold people away from the truth of the Word of God.

We need to quit accommodating our ungodly thoughts and release them!

> *God never hears your echoes. He only hears your voice.*

When an echo finds its way into our head, we need to cast it down. We'll talk more about that in upcoming chapters. We cannot hear clearly the voice of God through a muddle of echoes. And we cannot speak with the voice of faith when our ears are attuned to the past. God gives us a voice of faith, not to complain about our mountains or to bemoan the mountain we came from, but to tell our mountains to be removed.

If we believe the gospel of Jesus Christ, then we know that God instantly, wholeheartedly removes our guilt the minute we ask Him for forgiveness. Hear me now: *God never hears your echoes. He only hears your voice.* God is the only One who can forget something. He does it by doing away with it in the spirit. Our adversary, the devil, would love for us to think that heaven hears all the echoes of our minds. But when we have prayed and been dismissed from something by the blood of Jesus, the only thing that is left is an echo. If we will stand up and refuse to listen to the echoes of the mind, then God will establish in us the voice of the future. It's called *a voice of faith.*

- Faith calls the things that be not as though they are.

- Faith brings into being what God has already appropriated to us by grace.

- Faith is the voice that speaks tomorrow's realities into today.

- Faith is the voice that silences our echo chambers.

David discovered a principle that Christians in this generation need to get hold of: *Faith will never work in reverse. Faith that tries to work in reverse is fear.* Most people fear being disassociated from their past successes, and they fear duplicating their past failures. So they build walls around their lives, thinking they are hiding their failures and protecting their successes. In reality, they are shoring up their insecurities and strengthening their fear. It's a transparent wall to a person with a discerning heart. You see, the devil will use our successes and our failures to breed fear. "What if I don't live up to what I did before?" "What if I repeat this mistake?" The devil will use whatever angle is available.

If you are trying to duplicate your past, then you've lost your vision for tomorrow. If you are trying to escape your past failures, then almost without exception you are living under condemnation and guilt, which will lead to criticism, fear, rejection, bad doctrine, bad marriages, bad homes and bad everything. When you continually sow a seed of fear, you will ruin your life and miss your destiny.

I have seen whole nations of people rehearsing failures from the past. Every time I visit some places overseas all

I hear about is the past. The hurts, the wars, the pains, the hatreds, the animosity between religions and ethnic groups. How can the world know revival when people's minds are stuck in reverse? We will never have a move of God if we try to build on an echo.

I have seen churches being controlled by an echo coming out of a tombstone. They sing echo songs; they preach echo messages. They practice echo love, but they have not received a fresh word from the voice of God in fifty years. Men are dying and going to hell all around them, and they are completely missing His purpose.

God will establish in us the voice of the future. It's called a voice of faith.

How tragic to see people, churches and nations stuck in the past! Some echo chambers are so powerful in people's lives that you'd think they came complete with surround-sound speakers and sub-woofers.

A Changing Season

A move of God works only when the voice of faith speaks strongly into the present generation. The voice of the Word and of the Spirit of God mix together with our own spirits, and then people, churches and nations come alive in Him. When we rid our minds of echoes we can begin to speak with the voice of faith. We can say to the mountains of racism, drug and alcohol addiction, sectarianism, dead religion, false doctrines and cultism: "Be thou removed." Jesus said we should speak personally to the mountains of our generation and tell them to be removed and cast into the sea (Matt. 21:21).

An echo will never remove a mountain!

If God's people can get beyond their echoes, whole generations of people can have the move of God that He has planned for that generation. I believe this is happening today. Today we see the signs of Pentecost—healing, outpouring, prosperity—the signs and wonders that mark the beginning of every generational move of God. I believe we are in it right now. Something new is going on. There is a mighty outpouring of the Holy Spirit. Many streams are beginning to come together. But for God to accomplish all that He wants in this generation, we must look forward into His purposes, not backward into our pasts.

David recognized that he could no longer listen to the echoes of his past, whether they were failures or successes. He knew that to stay in step with God, he could not wake up in the echo chamber. He knew he had to get in God's time frame, forgetting yesterday and letting faith push him toward tomorrow.

What happened when David chose to wait in faith? God delivered him from his past, took him out of slow motion and put him on a path toward his destiny.

It is time to turn the echo chamber off and to cast down that imagination. Here's how David did it. He said, "And he hath put a new song in my mouth" (Ps. 40:3, KJV). Every generation has new songs that are songs of deliverance, songs of praise and songs that magnify God. Unharness your thoughts from the past, and allow God to renew your mind. He will put a new song in your mouth—a song that fits the time, the generation, in which He has called you to live.

David went on to say, "Many shall see it, and fear, and shall trust in the LORD" (v. 3, KJV). Your deliverance will cause someone else to get set free. When you stop living for the sound of echoes and start hearing and speaking with a voice of faith, people around you will "catch" what you've got.

There are voices beginning to rise up in this generation, and they are saying, "We are not controlled by echoes of success or failure. Exactly the opposite, we are pressing toward the mark, toward the prize, toward the high calling in Christ Jesus." There are teenagers who are suddenly beginning to see themselves as young men and women of God who will not be ashamed. When Jesus was going to go into Jerusalem, the children began to rejoice and say, "Hosanna, hosanna, hosanna, hosanna!"

> *For God to accomplish all that He wants in this generation, we must look forward into His purposes, not backward into our pasts.*

As Jesus was coming down the road, the disciples tried to keep the children away from Him, and finally He said, "Allow the children to come to me, and forbid them not!" (See Matthew 19:14.) Jesus loved the celebration of a new move of God.

In this book we're going to talk about living beyond yesterday—getting out of the echo chamber of the past, refusing to live in the basement of our lives and overcoming iniquity with the help of the Holy Spirit. In the upcoming chapters we'll look at this idea from several angles, digging into the Bible to help you understand what may be holding you back—and what you can do about it.

Because I believe that a revelation from God is always followed by a practical application, we'll also talk about specific ways to step out of yesterday and into God's powerful present purpose for your life. We'll look at the process the Holy Spirit uses to set us free from the past

as spelled out in God's Word. I believe God will powerfully set you free from the bonds of yesterday if you
accept His revelation to you and learn to live it out day
by day with His constant guidance.

Join me as we take this journey and begin living
beyond yesterday.

Chapter 2

Basement, Living Room and Rooftop Living

I BELIEVE THERE are three areas of the mind that we can choose to live in: the basement, the living room or the rooftop. The basement represents the past, the living room the present, and the rooftop the future. Each place has a function, but we have to spend the appropriate amount of time in each.

Living in the Basement

It's always cold in the basement, and you never know what spiders or creepy-crawly things have taken up residence since you last visited. The wooden stairs creak as you take each hesitant step, and the musty smell of yesterday envelops you like a worn-out old blanket. The walls and floor seem damp; there are cobwebs in all the corners, and the only light—a bare bulb hanging from a wire—does a less-than-adequate job of illuminating the place. After finding what you're looking for—a mop, an old yearbook—you hurry back up the stairs, pulling the string that turns the light off, and you shut the door behind you, hoping it will be a few years before you have to go down into your basement again.

Most houses have basements. They are places where we store things that have been given to us by friends or relatives—things we don't like and can't use, but we can't afford to get rid of them lest we offend somebody. Basements are where we keep things that once defined us—a childhood tricycle, a box of photographs, an old guitar—but no longer fit into our lives. A basement is like a clearinghouse for all our yesterdays.

My wife and I built a new home several years ago with a big basement for storage, but we don't like to go there very often. But what if the basement were our favorite room in the house? Imagine for a moment that my wife and I were to invite you to our house for dinner. You spend the afternoon getting ready, picking out the right clothes and putting on the right fragrance. At the proper time you show up at our house and ring the doorbell. We open the door and say, "So good to see you. Come right in. Can we take your coat? Terrific. Now follow us."

Then we open another door, pull a light string and walk you down into the basement. There we start opening boxes and showing you old trinkets. We talk and laugh about how it used to be. As you grow increasingly uncomfortable in the chilled, dimly lit room, we pull out pictures of people we used to know. With sober looks on our faces we talk about the bad things that have happened to us. Then we talk about regrets we have from our childhood. Box after box, memory after memory, until you decide the only way to get out of there is to pretend you have a headache and to ask permission to leave before dinner is served.

If we did this every time guests came over, people would begin to think there was something wrong with us—and rightly so. I don't care how pretty my house is on the outside, people would avoid socializing with us. "Don't go to the Hallam's," they'd say, "unless you want to spend an evening in their basement."

Some people spend the majority of their lives in the basement of their minds. Every conversation is filled with details about who has done them wrong. They say, "I've been hurt so many times in the past, and bless God, I'm so mad. Just pray for me that I'll make it to the end."

To borrow the term we used in the last chapter, they are living in the echo chamber of their minds.

Just as the basement in your home is the place you put things you don't want but feel obligated to keep, the basement of your mind is the place where you store things directly linked to your past and the choices you have made. Our pasts are full of things that happened to us that we wouldn't have chosen for ourselves—alcoholic parents, divorced parents, an ungodly father, an uncaring mother, kids at school who made fun of us—the list goes on. These are like the gifts people give you for which you have no use.

The basement of your mind is also full of bad decisions you have made—divorce, substance abuse, greed, ungodly living, sexual immorality. My point is this: Just because we go through the valley of the shadow of death does not mean we have to buy real estate there. Just because we've been through trauma doesn't mean we have to drag it up the basement steps every morning. Just because it happened in the past does not mean we have to live with it today.

> *Just because it happened in the past does not mean we have to live with it today.*

We need to understand that the power of the Holy Spirit not only saved our souls, but if we will apply the Word of God to our lives, His power will renew our minds. I'm not talking about locking up the past with its hurts inside and refusing to address it. I'm talking about putting our past in its proper place and, by the power of the Holy Spirit, taking control of our thoughts so that "yesterday" doesn't run the show.

Some psychologists may take issue with what I'm saying. They might say, "People can't let that stuff stew on the inside. They'll explode." But I believe many professionals lead people on a road to nowhere. They get them to drag everything from the basement up into the living room and sort through it day after day, week after week. But in the end they are worse off than before, because they have defiled their present with all these dusty, moldy boxes from the past—and they still have nowhere to put them.

Let me tell you about my 1975 Pontiac LeMans, a car I used to own. She had a 400-XY supercharged engine, and ran about 120 to 140 miles per hour. I kept that car—the pride of my youth—in top condition. One day, a tiny hole began to form in one of the glass packs on the muffler, so I took the car to a garage and left it to be repaired.

When I returned for the car and started home, I was shocked to discover that instead of fixing the glass packs, the garage mechanic had somehow completely dislodged the entire manifold exhaust system. Pipes were hanging loose and clanging as I drove home.

I learned that sometimes you can take your car to a local garage for minor repairs and wind up with worse problems than you had before you went there. If, however, you take the car back to the original manufacturer, who knows the car inside out, you will receive the help you need.

Going for counseling can sometimes be like that: You can end up with worse problems than you had before you went. Recently, I read some statistics that stunned me. A study revealed that of all the professions in the United States, psychiatry is a field in which a large number of suicides occur annually. Why am I telling you this? It seems to me that psychiatrists must be under a greater amount of oppression and deception than any other professional in the United States today.

Now, if you're a psychiatrist, please understand that I love you. If you are filled with the Holy Spirit, I know you must give godly counsel. But it shocks me to think there are men and women everywhere receiving counsel from individuals who are themselves on the very edge of losing it.

The basement exists for a purpose. It holds our past failures and successes. I am not saying we can forget every bad thing that has happened to us. We can't make ourselves have amnesia, but we can refuse to *dwell* in the basement. We can resolve to live in the living room of our lives. When an old thought comes our way we can examine it and say, "That belongs in the basement, and that's where it's going to stay."

Living in the Living Room

Now imagine that when you come over to our house for a visit, we open the door and escort you into our living room. There is a feeling of warmth and life in the home, and you sit on nice, new furniture. You look at the design of the interior and see that it isn't old and beat up, but new and well thought out. A fresh, pleasing color scheme has been added since the last time you were here. There are attractive portraits of our family on the wall and over the fireplace. The lights and music blend into an ambiance that puts you at ease and makes you feel as if you're in the very waiting room of heaven. The door to the basement is locked, and instead of talking about our yesterdays, we spend the evening talking about what God is doing in our lives today.

That's the kind of place you'd want to visit!

God made us to live in the present. We should spend most of our lives living in the living room.

God made us to live in the present. We should spend most of our lives living in the living room. Our living room defines who we are, both when we are alone and when we host other people. Have you noticed how living rooms reflect the personalities of their owners? Some people are always putting fresh new touches here and there or changing the color scheme every couple of years to match changing styles. When you walk in, you see immediately that things are different. Energy has been put into making the living quarters attractive. As a guest, you appreciate this. It shows that the owners are pro-gressing, learning and growing. It shows they know how to treat people well and how to create a welcoming atmosphere.

On the other hand, I'm sure we've all been to homes that never seem to change, not once a decade, not once a lifetime. The same orange shag carpet is on the floor; the same green couch and recliner are living out their days in front of the television. There are pictures of the kids on the walls from twenty years ago, and trinkets from vacations the family took in the 1960s. When you walk in, it's like being in a time warp. You almost want to react to the wasted potential of the home and the lack of care given to the appearance.

I'm not saying my style of living is better than another. God calls us to a diversity of lifestyles—spiritually as well as in the natural. We all will reflect Him in some unique way. Your living room and your life won't look like my mine. But we should all be continually cleaning and improving our spiritual living rooms. We ought to strive to live the kind of life that is encouraging—both to ourselves and to others—right here, right now.

Rooftop Living

Some people live in basements, others in living rooms and still others may choose to live on the rooftop. My house has a roof that is thirty feet high. I climb up there every now and then—I guess it's the little kid in me that misses climbing trees. I take a good long look at the horizon. On a clear day I can see forever. It makes me feel good to do that periodically. There, up on the rooftop, I see the big picture, the lay of the land, and I see where my house is in relation to everything around me.

Every now and then the Holy Spirit will take us up to the rooftop of our lives and give us a vision for down the road. No doubt you have experienced times like this. Maybe you go to the rooftop when the gifts of the Spirit begin to work or when the word of wisdom gives you understanding of what is coming next in your life. The rooftop is a place of vision. It's where we get a peek at what God has in store for us down the road.

Even our daily routines can include a moment on the rooftop. We can wake up praising God and let Him breathe fresh vision into us, even if we only expect a routine kind of day. The vision, the rooftop experience, is what keeps us pressing forward because we know that what's coming is better than what is behind us.

But we were not made to live on rooftops any more than we were made to live in basements. I love the view from my rooftop, but what if I went up and spent eight hours a day, seven days a week there? People would begin to wonder and talk about me. Instead of living in the present moment that God has given me, I would be trying to live constantly in the future.

I have met people who avoid living in today and act as if they are always on the rooftop. The problem is, if you stay up there too long, you start behaving in weird ways. Rooftop-dwellers stop taking care of the living room and the present concerns of the day. They always want to talk about what's coming,

> *The rooftop is a place of vision. It's where we get a peek at what God has in store for us down the road.*

many times giving people the impression they are super-spiritual and functioning on a different level than everyone else. Just as basement-dwellers become bound by their past, rooftop-dwellers get caught up in dreams of the future. Rooftop-dwellers are guilty of avoiding the present responsibilities of life.

I love it when the Holy Spirit gives me glimpses of what is yet to come, but I know that I cannot possibly live my daily routine on the roof. Someday, the dreams He has shown me will become a reality and become part of my day-to-day life in the living room. But until then, I must be content to live in the living room where the Lord teaches and guides me in my everyday routine through prayer, daily communion with God and informed preparation for the task at hand.

The Routine of Life

We have the choice of where we will live, and with the help of the Holy Spirit, we will find the right balance. The Holy Spirit always brings balance to the Christian life. He will not make you crazy, nutty or flaky.

> Blessed is the man that walketh not in the counsel of the ungodly, nor standeth in the way of sinners, nor sitteth in the seat of the scornful. . . . He shall be like a tree planted by the rivers of water, that bringeth forth his fruit in his season; his leaf also shall not wither; and whatsoever he doeth shall prosper.
>
> —PSALM 1:1, 3, KJV

These words from Psalm 1 say that those who will stay in the Word of God and walk upright will have good mental health. Their "delight is in the law of the LORD; and in his law doth he meditate day and night" (v. 2, KJV). The psalmist is talking about good mental health, balance and everything being ready in its season.

In the last chapter I used several verses from Psalm 40 to show how David was freed from his past. Verse 1 applies to living a balanced, living-room-centered life. David said, "I waited patiently for the LORD." This thought implies much more than sitting around believing that God will supply the answer. The word *patient* literally means "cheerful endurance." It does not mean sitting on the couch in a vegged-out state, but rather doing something active. The word *wait* actually means "consistency." It does not mean to sit on your thumbs. Rather, it would be like a waiter who goes through the process of serving a patron. When you go out to eat, the waiter comes up to you, greets you, takes your order, brings your dinner, checks back with you and makes sure you have everything you need for an enjoyable experience. He is a servant going through a routine of waiting.

The same meaning is conveyed in Psalm 40. David said that he consistently and routinely, with cheerful endurance, waited patiently upon the Lord. He achieved a balanced life. He didn't hide out in the basement. He didn't get skittish, like some believers do, and rush up to the roof-top uninvited to see if he could get a new revelation from God. He decided to live in the present moment, even if that meant there was less drama and emotion than he wanted. He decided to pray patiently, to be faithful in administering the business of the king, to be faithful in writing psalms and worshiping God. He didn't lay on his face all day sobbing about the past. He didn't go out and start a war to relieve his burdened heart. He simply decided to live in the moment God had given him and to carry out his duties both to God and men to the best of his understanding and abilities.

When I was a little boy, my daddy would tell me, "This afternoon I'll throw the baseball with you." I knew his word was good, and I could cheerfully endure going through the routine that I had in my life at that age because I knew that when Daddy showed up, he and I were going to play ball.

That's what living in the living room of our minds is all about: balance, perspective and a cheerful endurance for the Lord.

And the good news is this: The Bible says that when you wait upon the Lord, serving Him patiently and with cheerful endurance, He will set your feet upon a solid rock. He will set a pace for your life that is possible for you to maintain over the long term. He will establish your goings and cause your divinely given purposes to bear fruit.

Have you ever felt stuck in miry clay? Living the bal-anced life is the antidote for that. Miry clay gums up the routine of serving God, making it slow and somewhat ineffective. Maybe you have a roadrunner spirit but are like a tortoise in the follow-through. When you begin to shut out those echoes and live in the living room instead of the basement, God will put your feet on a paced lifestyle in Christ Jesus. David said, "I started cheerfully doing what God had told me to do, going through a whole new routine obeying God. When I did, I slammed the door on the basement of my adultery. I slammed the door on the basement of my failures. I slammed the door on the basement of all of my enemies that had come against me. I slammed the door on the fact that my brothers didn't like me that much. I shut the door on my past, and as I served God in the here and now, He set my feet on a rock."

Make an effort to live in your living room. Sometimes the Lord will call you up to the roof and give you visions of what is to come. Maybe occasionally life's circumstances will cause you to go into the basement. But you won't have to stay there long, and you can turn the light out when you leave.

Chapter 3

Blind Bartimaeus

ONE OF THE most outstanding examples of a person who shut off his echoes and climbed out of the basement is found in Mark 10. You may be familiar with the story of a blind man named Bartimaeus, but I want you to see it again in light of the first two chapters. I am always reading the Word, and I can think of no person in the Bible who showed more courage and determination to leave the past behind than Bartimaeus. The things he did to reach his miracle are practical steps that will help you walk out of the basement of your own life.

Jesus had come to Jericho, the place of the curse that is spoken about so much in Scripture. Someone who knows the history of Jericho might ask why Jesus bothered going there. God had levied a serious curse upon the city as well as those who might decide to live there. The Bible says that the man who rebuilt the walls back around Jericho would bury his oldest son when he laid the foundation and bury his youngest son when he hung the gate. (See Joshua 6:26.)

Yet the city obviously existed. It had been rebuilt in direct disobedience to God's command and was therefore under a curse. Still Jesus visited Jericho. What does this say to you and me? Listen closely because I want this to impart hope to you: God will send His Spirit, His Son and His presence to every cursed place on this planet. You may feel you are trapped in a cursed situation, but rejoice! God is not afraid of your problem or your circumstance. He will stride right through with confidence. And when you get a revelation of who He is, miracles will begin to happen. Your giant is no match for your stone!

Jesus was traveling with His disciples and a great number of people. There on the side of the road as they left the city was a man known as blind Bartimaeus. His name wasn't really "blind Bartimaeus," his name was Bartimaeus, but his problem literally had changed his identity.

> *God will send His Spirit, His Son and His presence to every cursed place on this planet.*

Isn't it just like humans to label people according to their shortcomings or sins? What if people referred to you as "Redheaded Sally" or "Old Fat Joe." Maybe you know people who carry nicknames through life because of a physical characteristic they may not even be able to control. Worse yet, maybe you know people who are defined by mistakes they have made. I hear people say, "There's that person who gossips all the time." "There's that former alcoholic." "There's that complainer." "There's that person who got a divorce." "Watch out for him; he's a problem person." We shove people into boxes and write them off, don't we?

Don't you wish more Christians would strive to be known as glorious people, those who are radiating the goodness of God? Don't you wish we would give each other nicknames that remind us of our identity in Christ? If you had to be identified with something, wouldn't you want it to be your joy, your peace, your wisdom in the Lord? I want a reputation that says I am a person who is constantly expecting God to work in my life and other people's lives. I want to be known for all the right things, not the wrong ones, and I want to see the people around me as moving beyond their pasts, not wallowing in them.

Nevertheless, Bartimaeus had been identified by the people around him. They gave him his reputation, drew a box around him and essentially said he would never go beyond his blindness. Not only that, but his problem had affected his own family. The Bible says, "Blind Bartimaeus, the son of Timaeus, sat by the road begging" (Mark 10:46). Even his father was now being labeled as a result of Bartimaeus's blindness. I have known entire families who have come to be identified by the same sin or personality trait. Their friends say, "Oh, those Smiths are such hotheads, from the grandfather on down." Usually traits (or identities) travel from father to son, but in Bartimaeus's case it went from son to father.

The Power of Hearing

Then something very important but very subtle happened. Bartimaeus *heard* that Jesus was passing by. Someone mentioned it to him, or he overheard a conversation people were having as they walked down the road. I believe that hearing was the first step Bartimaeus took in reaching his miracle.

Hearing is one of the most important activities in which we engage. What we hear forms what we believe and who we are. What you hear can change your life. That's why music is so important in shaping our character; we'll address that more in later chapters. When Bartimaeus heard that Jesus was coming by, he allowed that word to form in him the seed of faith. He decided right then and there that he was going to start climbing out of the basement. He heard the report and immediately started thinking differently about his future. I believe that faith welled up inside of him, and he saw that the chapters of his future could be rewritten. I believe he pictured in his mind a future spent not on the roadside begging, but on walking, talking, working, resting and worshiping like normal people of his day. I believe he saw himself being delivered from blindness. I believe he began to imagine himself free from his blindness. When you refuse to imagine God meeting your need, then your imagination has become your god.

Why do I believe this? Because I believe Bartimaeus not only heard that Jesus was coming, I believe he had a *Holy Spirit-inspired revelation of who Jesus was.* There were many people with Jesus that day, and they knew the historical fact that the man they were following was Jesus of Nazareth. Everybody knew that. A fact like that was a dime a dozen—common knowledge, not revelation knowledge. But when Bartimaeus heard that Jesus of Nazareth was coming, he had a flash of inspiration. Let me show you the sequence in the Bible.

> And when he heard that it was Jesus of Nazareth, he began to cry out and say, "Jesus, *Son of David*, have mercy on me!"
>
> —MARK 10:47, EMPHASIS ADDED

Bartimaeus heard that it was *Jesus of Nazareth,* but when the words came out of his own mouth they were "*Jesus, Son of David.*" A revelation happened inside of him that catapulted him past the historical facts into a new realm of spiritual insight that the rest of the religious onlookers that day lacked. The crowd knew Him as Jesus of Nazareth—an earthbound, geographical identity. But in that moment, Bartimaeus knew Him as the promised Messiah.

Just because you hear and know that Jesus of Nazareth is on His way does not complete the picture. Just because an unsaved person goes into a church and hears the gospel does not mean he will accept it. Why? Because the facts must be accompanied by the truth. Facts are facts, but the truth is a revelation only God can give. When you hear the Word and accept it in your heart, revelation can happen instantly to change your life forever. The blindest sinner on the street can see Jesus clearer than the religious person who appears to have perfect spiritual vision. The worst drug addict, the worst alcoholic, the worst person in prison can actually see Jesus as plain or plainer than the person who is doing the religious thing of the hour. Many religious people were hanging around Jesus that day to see if He would do some of His kingdom "tricks." They had no concept that He was God in the flesh. Religious people elbow around God to see what's going to happen, but they don't recognize who He is. A lot of people want the "shazam" and the spectacular, but they never get the supernatural. They're gawking around the move of God, and they go through life unchanged.

Bartimaeus saw past the religion. He heard about Jesus historically but talked about Him prophetically. He started yelling, "Jesus, Son of David, have mercy on me!" Suddenly the battle had begun between the voice of faith that was rising up in that poor beggar's throat and the echoes of his past that surrounded and defined him. The battle was on between Bartimaeus's reputation and his revelation.

Immediately, the people told him to quiet down. They were annoyed and perplexed at this man's persistence because they did not see what Bartimaeus saw. They echoed his echoes and tried to reestablish his reputation as a blind man with no future. It was as if someone had turned Bartimaeus's echo chamber on full blast as the crowd told him to shut his mouth.

Why was it OK for the religious leaders to spout their empty doctrine but not OK for the beggar to ask for deliverance? Why was it OK for the crowd to follow Jesus, pressing in on Him, but not OK for a blind man to use the only means he had—his voice—to get the Savior's attention? There are always two voices in the land. There are those who cry out by their revelation, and there are those who cry out for you to stop crying out by your revelation.

Religion is an echo, but revelation is a voice.

Everybody else was a spectator. Bartimaeus was a participator.

Everyone else had an opinion of Jesus. Bartimaeus had a revelation.

> *Religion is an echo, but revelation is a voice.*

Bartimaeus kept shouting all the louder, "Son of David, have mercy on me!" He let the voice of faith have the upper hand, and it began to drown out his echoes. I imagine that earlier in the day, when he heard that a large crowd was coming, he was overjoyed at the prospect of making a lot of money. After all, he was a beggar. Plying crowds from his roadside mat was his trade. So when his revelation of who Jesus was caused him to cry out, he must have felt the opposition, not just from the crowd but from the devil himself whispering into his ear, "You'd better shut up, blind man. You make your living off this crowd, and if you start upsetting them they won't give you a penny. They might even stone you."

But I can also imagine the voice of faith responding in Bartimaeus's heart, "This is not a good crowd from which to beg—this is a good crowd from which to get delivered. They're insisting you live up to your reputation as a blind beggar, but God wants to live up to your revelation instead. Get out of the echo chamber, Bartimaeus. Don't let these people stand in your way."

I'm telling you now, whenever you are on the brink of a miracle, people may oppose you. They might stand against the voice of faith they hear coming from your lips. But once you have a revelation of Jesus, nothing and no one can stop you from receiving what He has for you. Will it cost you your reputation? Maybe. Your livelihood? In some cases. Just bear in mind that usually others don't have your answer, and they don't want you to find it. They will echo your echoes, but you can respond with the voice of faith and revelation just as the blind beggar did.

God Hears Your Voice

God will never stop for an echo, but He will stop for a revelation. Jesus had already passed through town, but it was here, on the other side of Jericho, that the voice of faith apprehended Him.

> So Jesus stood still and commanded him to be called.
>
> —MARK 10:49

Suddenly, all eyes were on Bartimaeus. I can only imagine what was going through his mind. There he was, sitting and wearing his beggar's coat. He must have been

33

shaking, now the center of attention because the Master had called him. But what did he do? He threw aside his garment, rose and came to Jesus. His garment represented his occupation, his license to beg. Without it, he could not survive in that society. With it, he might survive. Not live, but simply survive. But he got rid of the limitation and the identification with his life as a beggar and walked boldly toward his deliverance. In essence he said, "I am not identifying with this coat anymore. This garment is my survival mode, but I am now in revival mode. Things are about to change." He came to Jesus, and as he stood before Him, he said, "Rabboni, that I may receive my sight" (v. 51).

Can you imagine the anticipation in Jesus' heart when, for the first time in who knows how long, He heard a man speak with the voice of faith—and it turned out to be a blind beggar? Everybody else was calling Him *Jesus of Nazareth*. Even His own disciples were having trouble understanding who He was. Yet here was a blind man saying, "Thou Son of David."

I can see Jesus looking at him and thinking, *Come on, Bartimaeus, don't drop the ball now. I'm about to unleash something that's going to make you an evangelist for all time. What you do today will be told for thousands of years to come.* I can also see the devil jump up on Bartimaeus's shoulder and say, "Bartimaeus, this is your chance to get rich. Tell Jesus that you want everybody in the crowd to give you five dollars. Tell him that you want a new suit of clothes and a new coat because yours is dirty and torn. With a new coat you can beg a little bit more." I can hear the echoes telling him to go back to his old profession, to forget taking the chance on God. But here was a man who had embraced a revelation in his heart and refused to listen to the echoes of his past. I can see him casting those thoughts down as he walked toward Jesus. I can see him thinking, *Today, alms aren't going to satisfy me anymore. I want my eyes back.*

> Then Jesus said to him, "Go your way; your faith has made you well."
>
> —MARK 10:52

In an instant, the power of God collided with Bartimaeus's faith. The echo chamber blew apart; the basement door swung wide open. The credits rolled on Bartimaeus's former life, and "Bartimaeus: The Sequel" began—only this time he had sight.

There is power when we stand up to our echoes! There is power when we say good-bye to the basement!

There is power when we stand up to our echoes! There is power when we say good-bye to the basement!

You do not have to be trapped in the past. You do not have to duplicate yesterday's failure. Somebody once said that history always repeats itself. Whoever said that didn't say it by the inspiration of the Holy Spirit. They said it by the intellectual experience of fallen man. The truth is, even with God, history doesn't always duplicate itself. Each day all things are new. Everything changes. You can start right where you are. You can be like Moses, who at eighty years of age shut up the echoes of the past and began to speak with a voice of faith. You can be like Caleb, nearly one hundred twenty years old and still pursuing the call of God. You can be like Joshua, who had a four-hundred-year heritage as a slave and in one night, because he believed the voice of God, became the leader of the greatest, richest nation and strongest military power that ever was. Or you could be like Bartimaeus, no longer blind because he believed the revelation he had of Jesus.

How does it happen? You start listening to the voice when everybody else is hearing an echo. There's always someone in the crowd who believes the voice of the Lord. Are you that person? The Holy Spirit will talk to you right where you are. Are you going to listen? Are you going to receive the revelation from God?

Let me ask another question. What blindness can Jesus remove from your life? Is it racism? Do you have a problem with regional pride and can't receive from somebody who speaks with a southern accent? Do you despise poor people? Rich people? People who have big degrees? People who don't have big degrees? Do you have a hard time accepting the younger generation? The older generation? Your parents? Your pastor?

What can Jesus do in your life to get your spiritual walk out of slow motion? How can He can take away your blindness? How can He awaken your dreams? Bartimaeus did what no one else did, and God called it faith. When you say, "I'll not live by the echoes anymore. I want the voice of God," you are setting yourself up for a miracle, just like the blind beggar. Follow the example of Bartimaeus. Don't let the jeers of the crowd get to you. Don't let faithlessness trip you up at the last minute. Press on until the Lord stops and calls you to Himself, and let Him heal you—forever.

Chapter 4

The Voice of Faith

WHY AM I so concerned about you shutting off the echoes of your past? Why do I want you to climb out of your basement and begin living beyond yesterday?

Is it because I want you to be happy? Yes, that's partly it. Is it because I want you to live free of the devil's attacks and fulfill your destiny? Yes, that's true. Is it because I want your life to be a lighthouse of hope that draws many to Christ? Yes, that's perhaps more true than anything.

But there is another reason. I believe that God is presently changing the season in which we live. There is a new generation emerging with unique purposes. I believe in dispensations of the Holy Spirit, and I believe there are numerous generations within each dispensation. A generation lasts around forty or fifty years, and every person reading this book will live in a part of at least three generations during his or her lifetime. We were born during one. We will live through another generation in its entirety, and then we will live in at least part of a third generation.

A generation has nothing to do with our age. A generation is the timing of God, a divine timespan where God works in a particular way. I'm not saying we can chart everything God does, but I do believe there are principles in the Word that help us understand the timing of God. If we tap into them, we won't struggle with our dispensation but will recognize the signs in our generation. When we recognize the signs, we stop being bewildered people watching history unfold and become participants and players who are actively making history.

We are about to arrive at the point where, as the body of Christ, we actually believe these things:

- We are the head and not the tail.
- We are above and not beneath.
- We are blessed coming in.
- We are blessed going out.
- We are blessed in the city.
- We are blessed in the field.

We are about to get to the point where we actually believe that our bodies are the temple of the Holy Spirit, and that greater is He who lives in us than he who is in the world.

We are not far from the point where we actually believe that with God nothing shall be impossible, and that if two or more of us touch on anything and agree, and ask it of our Father who is in heaven, we shall have the thing that we desire.

We are almost there, and people are getting glimpses of it now and then. We are moving into a new season in God, coming into a powerful time in the body of Christ at the inception of a millennium. We are not so much closing the tomb of the twentieth century as we are opening up the womb of the twenty-first century. Some people say the whole thing is about to wind up and that the world will end sooner, not later. If that's true, I'm out of here on the first bus. Just let Jesus punch my ticket, and I'll be gone when the trumpet sounds. But I think there is some time left, and in that time we have something very important and critical to do.

I believe that now are the greatest days in the body of Christ, and that we are called to

> *I believe that now are the greatest days in the body of Christ, and that we are called to participate in them.*

participate in them. God created us specifically for the work of this generation. We are some of the most blessed people in all of history to be living in the days in which we are presently living.

The Good Days

To participate in our purpose along with the rest of the body of Christ, we must learn to forget that which is behind and press toward the mark, the high calling of Jesus Christ. Our yesterdays were not the good old days. The Bible says, "Behold, now is the accepted time; behold, now is the day of salvation" (2 Cor. 6:2, KJV). Never before have so many people turned to Christ, received healing and been set free from the bondages of Satan.

There is a move of God that has already broken upon our land that will rival what took place at the beginning of the twentieth century. The revival we are moving into will be many times greater than that which took place at Azusa Street. That revival, led by the great man of faith William Seymour, continues to change the course of history. It literally split the twentieth century wide open as the Holy Spirit poured out of Himself in a way people had not seen for centuries.

But God wants us to live in the now. We can't live in Azusa Street anymore. God knew this generation needed you. Get out of yesterday, out of the basement of failure and success, and come into what God is doing right now. It has nothing to do with your age, whether young or old. If you are alive, you qualify.

If anybody in the Bible ever got involved with a coming move of God, it was David. As a teenage boy, he was positioned for a move of God that did not happen until a few years later. As a result, when everyone else was demoted, he was promoted. Why? Because David quit listening to his echoes and waited patiently for the move of God. There is a sense in which we need to streamline our routine, growing and learning in God, so that when the move comes upon us, we are not found lacking. Remember that waiting on the Lord is not passive but active, and it means maturity, a renewing of the mind, a belief that God will guide us.

David could sense in his spirit that God was doing something new. He didn't always know how to get into it, but he could tell that God was preparing to pour out a wave of His glory. Throughout the Bible, godly men could sense a coming move of the Holy Spirit. Hebrews 11 talks about people who sensed it in the spirit.

We are living in a day where there is a mighty move of the Holy Spirit. There are things that can enhance our moving into what God is doing in this particular hour. But there are things that can be limitations or barriers. We want to know how to get into the move.

The Voice of Faith

To be part of this move of God, it is critical that we understand the voice of faith and the mind of the King. Speaking with the voice of faith is one of the most important kingdom principles found in the last chapter. We saw how Bartimaeus spoke with a voice of faith, which silenced his echoes and brought him a miracle. What is the voice of faith? Where does it come from? How does it operate in our lives?

Faith, the Book of Hebrews tells us, is the evidence of things not seen (Heb. 11:1). I personally believe that everything God said He would do for humanity has already been done. Faith makes a demand of all that is laid up in store for you and me already. I believe faith is like having an access card to the benefits of God. It is the hand that reaches into heaven's provision, takes hold of an answer in the spiritual realm and will not let go until the answer is pulled down into the manifestation realm. For instance, if you are sick in body, the Bible says that by His stripes you were healed (1 Pet. 2:24). Healing is for the child of God and is accessible to you and me. Faith comes from hearing the Word of God, believing it and getting hold of the healing portion for your life. When you have a hold on it, you should start saying, "I have it," because you will. We call that "holding fast to the confession of our faith" without wavering. (See Hebrews 10:23.)

I have found out that everyone believes in confession in one form or another. Some people believe in confession of their faith. But others confess all the time how sick they are—and as a result, they are always sick. Somebody once told me, "Don't tell me all that faith stuff; just tell me the facts."

I replied, "The facts will kill you."

Some people are walking "facts" machines, but facts

won't do anything for you. More than facts, you need the truth. The truth is what sets you free. The fact is, you might be sick in your body. The truth is that by His stripes you were healed. In the kingdom of God, the truth always overrides the facts. Everything we consider factual isn't necessarily the truth. It's a fact that Goliath said, "Today, I'm going to feed your carcass to the fouls of the air." But his words, in the end, were not the truth. It's a fact that you might not have enough money, but the truth is "my God supplies all of my needs." (See Philippians 4:19.) It depends on what you're going to believe. Are you going to believe the facts? Or are you going to believe the truth, which is the Word of God? Faith will create your answer and set it in motion.

Your Problem Has a Time Limit

One day as I was reading, the Holy Spirit said to me, "The devil has a time limit on him." Every affliction that comes on you has a time limit on it. Bartimaeus's blindness had a time limit on it, though he had to apprehend the miracle to bring that spiritual truth into the factual realm. The devil, the source of affliction, is not an eternal creature like God. The devil is still limited to time. Once demons spoke to Jesus through two possessed men and said, "Why do You come to torment us before our *time?*" (See Matthew 8:29.)

Paul reiterates that any problem that comes against us has a time limit on it: "Our light affliction, which is but for a moment . . ." (2 Cor. 4:17). When we speak with the voice of faith, we can rightly say that every affliction is bound by time and will fall away from us.

So, the way to overcome fear is with faith. But there is no such thing as faith without confession. Look through the Bible and try to find faith that works without your willingness to say it with your mouth when you believe it in your heart. You won't see it. The way you destroy the echoes is to say the opposite of what fear is saying. When fear says something bad will happen, say, "I believe it's the other way around. Something good will happen because God is at work in this situation, and an answer is on the way."

I don't care how good it is for you right now; it can only get better tomorrow in the kingdom of God. There are no lesser days in the kingdom. It never gets worse— it always gets better. I'm not saying we won't have challenges. Challenges come and go, but the glory remains. The joy remains. The Bible says we go from glory to glory, not from glory to defeat. We go from good to better.

In Romans 4:17, God calls the things that be not as though they are. And Jesus said "The works I do, you'll do it even greater." (See John 14:12.) So we do not call things that are as though they are not. We call things that are not as though they are.

> For our light affliction, which is but for a moment, worketh for us a far more exceeding and eternal weight of glory; while we look not at the things which are seen: for the things which are seen are temporal; but the things which are not seen are eternal.
>
> —2 CORINTHIANS 4:17–18, KJV

An Example

Many hundreds of times I have seen how the voice of faith can reverse a seemingly impossible reality. One time a lady in my church was riding a horse when the horse spooked and ran into an oak tree. She hit a limb, broke her spine and her neck in two places and became instantly paralyzed. The doctors now call it the "Christopher Reeve injury." She was rushed to the hospital where the doctors gave her a very negative prognosis.

The family called me on Friday afternoon, and I went to see them in the hospital. Robin was laid out on a board with a halo screwed into her head. She could barely breathe and could not move. She could only move her eyes from side to side. I cried because I love these people. When I came in, I leaned down beside her and said, "Robin, Jesus is Lord."

The first thing she said to me was, "Pastor, this is going to be a great testimony for God."

We were in the middle of the worst news imaginable. Her x-rays were there on a lit screen. It made your blood run cold to see them. Her brain was trying to swell. Her husband was standing there, his eyes red and weary. I remembered two years earlier I had called that woman out and prophesied to her and said, "God will use you in a healing ministry."

Faith doesn't remove all the questions, but it sure removes all the doubt. I said, "Robin, they'll only let us in here for a minute or two, so let me pray for you right now." We laid hands on her and prayed, spoke the Word of God and refused to be moved off our faith. Our emotions were very vulnerable—we hurt. But we were praying in faith through our tears of anguish. People from our church set up a prayer vigil in a nearby room.

That night about 11:30, I had a strong unction in my spirit to go back and pray for her again. Jesus prayed for people more than once, and I think He prayed in faith every time. When I arrived, Robin's husband and others were still in the room. By this time Robin was sedated and did not even know we were in the room. I laid hands on her again, obeyed the Holy Spirit, prayed the prayer of faith and left. That was about midnight on the day of the accident.

The next morning I received a phone call. "You might want to come down to the hospital," Robin's husband said.

Not knowing what he meant, I said, "I'll be there as soon as possible." When I got there, everybody's face was lit up. I looked on the wall and saw her x-rays. Next to them was a second set. They had taken her back for more CAT scans to determine the injury to the brain. When they looked at the report, they noticed that her spine was totally lined up. Feeling had begun to return to her hands and feet.

A week or so later she walked out of the hospital totally healed. There are still no side effects today.

I printed both x-rays in our newsletter, along with these words: "The doctors told us this was a 'Christopher Reeve' injury, but Jesus is stronger than Superman."

Power in the Tongue

We prayed with the voice of faith over Robin, and she was healed. We spoke the solution and received it, in Jesus' name. We confessed and apprehended the answer.

Some are constantly talking the problem—not the solution. The Bible, in both the Old and New Testaments, explicitly warns about the power of the tongue. God admonishes us to guard our tongues. It is with the tongue that we both bless and curse. It is with the tongue that we confess Jesus Christ as Lord and Savior.

Some are constantly talking the problem—not the solution.

What words are coming out of your mouth minute by minute, hour by hour, day by day? If you were to have a tape recording of all that you have said so far today, what would it sound like?

I grew up in a family of seven children. My daddy drove a laundry truck for sixty-five dollars a week. We were so poor that the poor people called us poor. It was not until much later that I realized how poor we were when I was growing up. Yet not once did Daddy ever call us poor. I never heard him speak it. Daddy always tithed and gave his offerings to the church, and today he's a rich man. He did not perpetuate poverty by helping to speak it into existence.

I have three daughters and a tremendous wife, and my daughters know how to get what they want out of me. They know that if they come and beg me for something, they cannot have it, because I'm not raising beggars. They have to come to me with confidence and look me in the eye when they ask. If they come with their heads down, the answer is no. They know it. That's the way it works in my house. They don't get anything at the back door. If they try to manipulate me, I know immediately that something is wrong. My girls were taught to look me in the eye and speak with faith. God says to come boldly before His throne. Each of my girls has her daddy figured out. Each will come in, kiss me on the cheek and say, "Hey, Dad, can I do this or do that?"

"All right, how much do you want?" I will respond. I'll let them do just about anything if they come with the right attitude, because I want them to understand the power of words spoken in faith.

Mark 11:23 is a powerful teaching. In it, Jesus says:

> For assuredly, I say to you, whoever says to this mountain, "Be removed and be cast into the sea," and does not doubt in his heart, but believes that those things he says will be done, he will have whatever he says.

I learned a long time ago that anytime God said something, He said it for a reason. If God said that whoever would say to the mountain, "Be removed and cast into sea," would have whatever he asks, then it tells me that it can work for us. I'm glad that He went on to say:

> Therefore I say to you, whatever things you ask when you pray, believe that you receive them, and you will have them.
>
> —MARK 11:24

When do you have them? When you pray and believe. I am so glad that Jesus did not turn to Peter that day and say, "I want you to understand, don't ever try this. This is strictly one of those kingdom tricks. You have to have lived in heaven for this to work. Only I can speak to mountains and tell them to be removed. This will not work for you, nor for any other people who will come after you. So do not try this yourself, Peter, whatever you do."

I'm so thrilled that Jesus said, "Whoever will say to this mountain..." You and I are "whoever." Your mountain needs to recognize the authority of the Holy Spirit in your voice. You need to learn how to speak to that mountain. Jesus said there will be mountains and there will be mountain movers—and I want to be in the mountain mover crowd. The voice of faith says, "I hear all of these echoes coming at me, but this is how it's going to be, mountain. I'm going to tell you to leave in Jesus' name, and I'm going to believe that you are gone the moment I say it. When I open my eyes, I don't care what I see. As far as I'm concerned, you're gone; you're dead; your roots have dried up."

That is the voice of faith. That is how a king thinks.

We've got to get out of this "Woe is me; the devil has been after me all day" mentality. We have to stop tucking our chins against our chests when we ask God for something. Scripture says, "By the one man's offense death reigned" (Rom. 5:17). But the same verse also says, "Much more those who receive abundance of grace and of the gift of righteousness will reign in life through the One, Jesus Christ." The righteousness of which that verse is speaking is literally the removal of all guilt, doubt, condemnation, fear, intimidation, inferiority and *everything else* in your inner man that keeps you from standing before God like an upright son or daughter. Anything that keeps you from boldly coming before the throne of grace and obtaining help in a time of need is not of God. I no longer want death reigning in my life, so in the name of Jesus, I'm going to keep speaking with the voice of faith, and I'm going to have an abundance of grace and righteousness in my understanding.

Every demon in hell knows you are stronger than they are. Get out of the game of always trying to decide which obstacles in your life are of God or which are not of God. Decide that any obstacle you see will be overcome in the name of Jesus. Get an abundance of grace and righteousness to fill your mind so you will say, "I'm going to reign in life through Jesus Christ, and I don't care if there are walls of Jericho in front of me or if I face the lion's den or prison. It makes no difference. I'm coming out of that thing when it's all over. I'm going to deal with it in the spirit and keep on going. I'm not going to let something captivate my whole life and sidetrack me from my destiny in God."

I heard a story once about a man who bought a big stallion. That was the good news, because he'd always wanted a horse. Then his son got on it, the horse threw the boy, and he broke his arm. That was the bad news. But there was a war going on, and then, a draft. Because of the broken arm, the boy wasn't able to go into war. That was good news. The point is, if you judge a circumstance by its appearance, you will probably get it wrong, because from different angles it can look like a blessing or a curse. You can't judge everything on one simple thing. You have to say, "Wait a minute, my life is in the hand of God. I'm going to rule and reign in life through Jesus Christ. I don't care what comes or what goes. Before this thing is over, God will get the victory out of it."

The Mind of the King

To learn to speak with the voice of faith, as Bartimaeus did, we need to look at the example of Christ. Our King spoke and acted with more faith than anyone who ever lived. Philippians 2:5 says, "Let this mind be in you which was also in Christ Jesus." God said that we are kings and priests unto our God (Rev. 5:10). Jesus is the original King and Priest, and we are made in His likeness and image. To understand the voice of faith, we need to understand the mind of the King whom we serve and think the way He thinks.

If you think about it, had He not been the Son of God, Jesus' own upbringing and origins would have made Him a good candidate for the devil's inferiority and condemnation. His birth was surrounded by apparent scandal. He wasn't from a very flashy town. One individual remarked scornfully, "Can anything good come out of Nazareth?" (John 1:46). But Jesus stayed focused on His *destination,* not His *origination.* He was always pressing forward, even to the brink of forgetting His mother (Matt. 12:48). Of course we know He didn't forget her, but the point is still powerful. He was looking ahead—not behind. If the devil could have gotten Jesus wrapped up in the echoes, it would have been over, but Jesus didn't listen to the echoes. He listened to faith—and He spoke with a voice of faith 100 percent of the time.

In Matthew 15 there is a story that shows us how the voice of faith operates.

> Then Jesus went out from there and departed to
> the region of Tyre and Sidon. And behold, a woman
> of Canaan came from that region and cried out to
> Him, saying, "Have mercy on me, O Lord, Son of
> David! My daughter is severely demon-possessed."
> But He answered her not a word. And His disciples
> came and urged Him, saying, "Send her away, for
> she cries out after us."
>
> —MATTHEW 15:21–23

When you get a revelation, it is not an opinion. When
a person gets a revelation from God, as Bartimaeus did, I
don't care if Jesus doesn't answer you; you keep talking
to Him anyway. Revelation never says, "Well, I guess this
faith stuff doesn't work." Faith knows who holds the
answer. It doesn't make any difference if everybody
around you says, "No, no, no." Faith wells up and says,
"Yes, yes, yes."

I used to wonder why Jesus didn't say a word to this
woman. I finally came to the conclusion that Jesus was
testing His disciples to see if any of them had received
the revelation of who He was. When He finally answered
her, I believe He was speaking to His disciples. You see,
when Jesus came to the earth, He did not go call a hundred thousand people around Him. He called twelve very
dysfunctional people with little or no revelation of anything, and He began to teach them to speak with the
voice of faith.

> But He answered and said, "I was not sent except to
> the lost sheep of the house of Israel."
>
> —MATTHEW 15:24

Jesus was saying, "Wake up, disciples! I'm sent to the
lost sheep. I'm trying to get Israel saved, but Israel is
rejecting Me."

Then she came and worshiped Him, saying, "Lord,
help me!"

—MATTHEW 15:25

She refused to be denied, even though, in my view,
Jesus hadn't spoken to her yet. She went right through
that fisherman. She went right past that tax collector,
aiming for her answer.

But He answered and said, "It is not good to take
the children's bread and throw it to the little dogs."
—MATTHEW 15:26

The word *dog* here is not a derogatory term. If we
were reading the original Greek rendering, it says, "It is
not correct to take a child's food and give it to its pet."
Jesus was saying, "It's not right to feed your puppy before
you feed yourself."

And the woman responded, "That's true, Lord, but
even the pets eat the crumbs that fall from their master's
table."

It's important to understand that Jesus was not putting this woman down. He was talking about something
much deeper than those thick-headed disciples could
understand. He was talking to someone who had revelation knowledge and knew that He had come to save
Israel. He was telling her, "I know you're not Jewish, and
it's not right for Me to minister to the non-Jewish people
before I minister to the Jewish people." But He said it in
a way that caused her faith to explode and a bulldog
tenacity to come alive in her. She suddenly became, if I
can say it, a pit bull in the Holy Spirit. She was fixing to
bite on to His anointing and not let go until He blessed
her.

I have a yellow Labrador retriever that stays in a
kennel built behind my garage. I play with her a time or

two a day, and sometimes I like to look at her because she's a pretty yellow dog. I'll step out on the back porch and call her, and even though I can't see her, a minute later there she is, happy as can be. That's kind of the way faith works. Some people need to grow up in their faith and start calling those things that be not as though they are. My dog is not visible to me when I call her, but I know that if I call her she's going to come. Faith says, "Jesus is the Lord. He is the healer. He is the Savior. I'm going to call my healing today."

> And she said, "Yes, Lord, yet even the little dogs eat the crumbs which fall from their masters' table." Then Jesus answered and said to her, "O woman, great is your faith! Let it be to you as you desire."
>
> —MATTHEW 15:27–28

Her faith apprehended the answer she sought. The voice of faith flipped on the power switch and caused an answer to come. I like the way the King thought. He always spoke to people's revelation, and He could only speak to them at the level of their revelation. When I study Jesus, one of the things I see is that He saw everything as living. The only thing that at one time He didn't see as living was a fig tree (Matt. 21:18–20). Although the fig tree had leaves, it bore no fruit. So He said, "Let no fruit grow on you ever again," and the fig tree withered away. In essence, Jesus was saying to that impotent fig tree: "You are not bearing fruit, so be plucked up, and I will plant something else in your place." He saw everything as alive. Everything is powerful. Everything has potential.

In Matthew 15 the little Gentile woman came walking up to Jesus with no rights in the Old Covenant of Israel. But she literally leapt over a dispensational chasm and jumped into a New Testament revelation. She was bold enough to say, "I know that I'm not Jewish, God, but that doesn't make any difference, because You're still the Lord. I'm still one of the things that You created. So, feed me, Lord."

It's important to get that kind of faith to well up inside you, too. You may not think you are anything special, but you are made in the likeness and the image of God. You have a right and a reason to ask Him

> *When your revelation is larger than your problem, you are at the door of breakthrough.*

for bread. All you need is a revelation. I don't know if your problem is big or little, if your daughter is vexed with a devil or your car won't start in the mornings. But, like Bartimaeus and this woman, when your revelation is larger than your problem, you are at the door of breakthrough. It will happen at any moment. You can leave that car sitting in your driveway, go back to the house, get a phone call and find that someone has given you a car. Maybe you say, "That can't happen that way." If that's what you need, it can.

I can't help but think of Nelson Mandela, former president of South Africa. He had incredible tenacity. He felt the political system was wrong, and he went to prison for it. He was willing to die for his cause. They stuck him in prison for many years. Yet the moment he got out, he started speaking those same values that he had when he went in. His revelation of what he wanted to change was that strong.

Thank God when Christian men and women get a similar revelation of what Jesus did for us at Calvary!

Why We Call on God

There are three reasons people call on God. The first reason is *the burning bush experience.* Some people have to have God knock them upside the head in the desert before they get a revelation of Him. God sets a bush on fire, and it's so real, so plain, it's undeniable.

The second reason is *a burning house experience*, such as when an emergency strikes—an illness, a financial shortage, a relationship problem. Your house is on fire and about to collapse all around you. People call on God in those times.

The third reason is *a burning heart experience.* That is when you get up in the morning with your heart burning to know God more. I read about D. L. Moody, the great preacher of yesteryear. He was a great and powerful man. Even in his day a thousand people would come out to hear him when he spoke about Jesus. At one time he was asked, "How do you get all of these people to come out here and listen to you speak?"

He said, "Before I go out and preach, I get in a little place by myself, and I say, 'God, set me on fire.'"

Someone asked me once why I shout at times when I preach. It's because I'm on fire! I can't help it. When you get a burning heart, the Word of God becomes like fire on the inside, and you will not be denied.

Working Backward From the Answer

It's very important to realize that when you have a need, Jesus has the answer. You ask, "Do I have to beg God for the answer?" No, you don't. But you may have to hold on until the answer gets there. You may have to go through one or more stages on the way to your victory.

I believe that Jesus sees every problem from the point of view of the answer. I also believe that no problem is too big or too small for Him. The same voice of faith will activate the answer.

In Matthew, we read about a time when Jesus had compassion on a whole multitude—just as He did on one Gentile woman. He called His disciples to Himself, and said to them:

> I have compassion on the multitude, because they have now continued with Me three days and have nothing to eat. And I do not want to send them away hungry, lest they faint on the way.
>
> —MATTHEW 15:32

As Jesus looked at the multitude, those for whom He had no personal responsibility, He saw their need as important. To a king, every need has some degree of importance. Jesus never despised little things, and He never felt intimidated by large things. In one instance it was one lone woman who needed her daughter healed. He didn't despise that. On another instance it was the multitude who had been with Him as He healed and taught for three days. Neither did He despise their need. Jesus looked out on the multitude and had compassion on them.

Recently as I was studying this story, the Holy Spirit said, "If you are going to think like a king, you're going to have to learn how to have compassion on the multitude. Anybody can have compassion on one person. You have to learn to love the multitude the same way you love the individual."

How true that is. Anybody alive can have compassion on one other person. That's a standard-issue human emotion. You don't have to be saved and filled with the Holy Spirit. For example, it's easy to feel compassion for one baby. But if you look at a whole nursery of crying babies—what do you feel then? In a sense, Jesus looked at the "nursery" of mankind and had compassion on every one of them, including you and me. He looked on the multitude and loved every soul to the same degree that He loved John.

Because of the day we live in right now, the multitude needs the compassion of the Holy Spirit. God will let you minister to a multitude just as Jesus did.

> Then His disciples said to Him, "Where could we get enough bread in the wilderness to fill such a great multitude?"
>
> —MATTHEW 15:33

We should never look at things from the point of the problem, but from the point of the answer. We should start from the answer and work backward. I contend that Jesus saw every need as met. When He saw these four thousand men, plus their wives and children, He did not see them as hungry. He saw them fed; He saw the answer.

> *We should never look at things from the point of the problem, but from the point of the answer. We should start from the answer and work backward.*

The disciples did not. They saw it as more work, more problems, more time, more energy. The size of the need was a problem to His disciples, but to Jesus it gave a reason for showing them again how to speak and act with the voice of faith. Peter may have looked at Him and said, "Where are we going to get this kind of food?" But Jesus knew that the bigger the problem, the bigger the answer.

Big answers begin small. Some time ago I read about a man who owns expensive resort hotels in Hawaii. He was interviewed about where he got his start, and he said, "I was a short-order cook in a cheap restaurant. My job was to cook breakfast. All I did was make pancakes, flipping them one at a time. Then I decided that I could do this for myself, so I got my own little place, and I started flipping pancakes and selling them." Then he said, "I've gotten to where I am today one flip at a time."

Jesus didn't start with much more in the way of resources than that resort owner had—a few pieces of bread. I've noticed that Jesus always assessed His resources and never mocked that with which He had to work. The tendency of the masses is to doubt. "How are we going to feed all these people? Where do you expect us to get all this food?" That's why opinion polls offer no vision. The opinion of the masses almost always goes toward doubt and mediocrity.

When you begin to speak with the voice of faith, you must be willing, as Jesus was, to stand alone. Jesus looked at twenty thousand hungry faces and twelve doubting disciples, and Jesus knew He was the only one offering an answer. There will be times when you have to be willing to stand alone, if necessary, to get God to work for you.

We all know what happened that glorious day on the hillside with Jesus. Thousands received a miracle meal, and the rest of us got an enduring lesson on faith.

The next time you have an impossible situation facing you, do not cave in, back off, shut down, turn around, run off, faint, fear, backslide or anything else. Instead, why not speak with faith? The next time a doctor says you have a physical problem, don't blaspheme God. Don't cry. Don't say, "I tried that faith stuff, and it doesn't work." Don't get mad at the doctor. Don't start cursing.

But say, "In the name of Jesus, I will live and not die. Greater is He who is in me than he who is in the world. Sickness, sit down." Instead of getting upset because someone else was healed and you haven't received your healing yet, take control.

If we are going to succeed in living beyond yesterday, we have to employ the voice of faith, not just in extraordinary circumstances, but every day . . . even every hour. Are you ready to answer back to your echoes, stand alone in faith, speak your solutions and apprehend your answers? In the next section, we will see how standing on God's Word and speaking with the voice of faith will help us to overcome our most entrenched sin habits and echoes.

PART
Two

Chapter 5

Bruised for Our Iniquity

SOMETIMES WHEN WE talk about echoes of the past, we are talking about one-time mistakes we made. Other times, however, we mean a repetitive pattern of sin ingrained in us like oil in a leather baseball glove. Perhaps you've observed someone whose sin problem kept them from maturing in God. Or maybe you have known the desperation of a vice that seemed impossible to defeat.

Let's move to deeper waters—beyond the things that have happened to us that cause us to live in the past. Now we will look at the very root of our sin nature, what the Bible calls *iniquity*. Here we will take on the echo machine itself. These pages have the power to change your life forever, and I pray that the Lord will speak to you about overcoming your own areas of iniquity.

Repetitive Sin

A few years ago—even before I became a pastor—the

Lord began to deal with me about the subject of iniquity. It has since become the most-requested subject on which I have ever been asked to preach. I have discovered that many Christians who sincerely love Jesus Christ are constantly tripped up by repetitive sin. These individuals seem to have placed everything about their lives under the blood of Christ except one or two areas that seem constantly to cause them trouble. These one or two things keep cropping up throughout their lives, creating havoc and keeping them from living in the total victory promised to Christians in the Word of God.

Every time these individuals appear to be getting ahead in the things of God, these particular problem areas surface again, rearing their ugly heads, so to speak—and all spiritual progress is suddenly lost. Those old sin problems seem to reach right out, grab them and drag them down. Perhaps you know what I'm talking about.

The Bible repeatedly mentions iniquity, and yet iniquity is an area in which many modern-day Christians seem to lack spiritual insight and understanding. I did not understand iniquity until the Holy Spirit began to deal with me about it. In fact, it's doubtful that I would even have entered the ministry unless God *had* dealt with me about iniquity. In order to answer the call of God on my life, I had to first deal with some iniquity in my own life.

Today there is much teaching in the body of Christ on the subject of generational curses—not necessarily a scriptural term. The thought is right, but the terminology is not. I believe the term God uses to describe what some call "generational curses" is *iniquity*. It's why the children of Israel repeatedly fell into the same kinds of sins. (See Exodus 34:7.) It's why even today some people get hooked up to God, only to fall into the same sin trap that plagued their lives before salvation—the same sin trap that habitually ensnared their ancestors.

But I have good news. Isaiah 53:5 says that Jesus *was wounded for our transgressions.* Transgressions—that's sin. It also says that He *was bruised for our iniquities.* Iniquities—that's those inherent weaknesses, or propensities, in the soul or mind toward sin that keep tripping up some Christians. The good news is that the work of Jesus upon the cross at Calvary has already purchased freedom from sin and victory over iniquity.

It's a Gene . . . Isn't It?

Did you know that everything about you physically is inherited? Scientific studies have shown that the same human genes are reproduced repeatedly, over and over again, from one generation to the next, perfectly passing down traits ranging from hair and eye color to height to personality quirks—even handwriting.

We are the sum total of our mothers and our fathers and their mothers and fathers before them, genetically speaking. Scientists agree on it, and nowhere in the Bible is this concept contradicted. In fact, it is reinforced in the pages of the Bible—a book that has always had a great deal to say on the subject of inheritance. We might even say that the Bible is the "family tree" of every believer, tracing our heritage back to our first parents, Adam and Eve, in the Garden of Eden.

When someone remarks about how much you resemble a parent or a sibling, have you ever chuckled, then commented, "It's in the genes"? I have. It's a common response to such observations, but I want to point out that there's a whole lot more to this issue of inheritance than meets the eye.

Those Red-Haired Hallams

I have red hair and blue eyes. My mama and daddy have

red hair and blue eyes. Most of my grandparents had red hair and blue eyes. I have six brothers and sisters, and most of them have red hair and blue eyes, too. In fact, I have forty-some kinfolk who have red hair and blue eyes.

If you grew up in my family and didn't have red hair and blue eyes, the rest of us got very suspicious. Why? Because red hair and blue eyes are two traits we inherited. There's no telling how many Hallams before us have had red hair and blue eyes. It's a part of who we are.

My daddy is seventy years old now, but by his voice you couldn't tell it. When you talk to him on the phone, you might think you were talking to me because our voices sound so much alike. Sometimes people will phone and, when I answer, ask, "Is this Bill Hallam?"

I'll say, "No—this is Walter." They're always surprised at how alike Daddy and I sound on the phone. Why is that? He passed the trait that distinguishes the sound of his voice down to me. I inherited it. I don't know how he did it, but I know it happened. I have Daddy's voice.

I also have this funny little crook in my little finger. It sticks out, but it comes in handy when I'm playing the piano and trying to reach those C and F keys way down on the other end of the keyboard. That little crooked finger comes in handy for a lot of other things, too. It's great for holding a baseball. And one time somebody even told me, "When you point that finger when you preach, I think God is pointing at me."

But when Mama holds her hand up, anyone can see that she has the same crook in her little finger, just like mine. I don't know how she got it. But I know how I got it. I inherited it from Mama.

Not Just Physical Traits Are Inherited

Yes, there's more to inheritance than meets the eye. While some inherited traits are easy to spot outwardly, other things are less readily apparent. To spot those traits, a person needs to be around someone for a period of time to observe all the similarities.

Take handwriting, for instance. Many years ago during a visit to my Grandmother Hallam's house in Beaumont, Texas, my father was rummaging around in her attic. He found this old trunk, and inside it he found this old slate that had big, pretty handwriting on it. He asked his mother, "When did I write that? When I was a boy?"

But she said, "Son, that's not your handwriting—that's your daddy's handwriting." Now, that's really interesting, because my grandfather died due to a railroad accident when Daddy was just two years old. Yet Daddy's handwriting is just like his daddy's—big and pretty. How did that happen? Daddy inherited his style of handwriting from his father.

Experts will tell you that handwriting has a lot to do with a person's personality. Did you know that even personality traits are passed on? There's a couple in our church who each have electrifying personalities. This couple lights up the whole room, and it's hard to conceive of them ever having had a bad day in their lives. I've met their two sons, and they are exactly like their mom and dad. You can't help but love them. Since I am a student of human nature anyway, it always fascinates me to encounter people like this family and to see the uncanny similarities between the personalities of parents and their children.

My wife and I have three daughters. One of our daughters is just like me, but one of them is just like my wife—so much so that it's uncanny. She walks like my wife, talks like my wife, acts like my wife.

The scientific community calls it *genetics*. The Bible calls it *inheritance*. Whatever it's called, it's real.

It's even incredible how the soulish realm is passed on via inheritance. How many of you who are parents seem to know what your children are thinking? Why? Because you've been there before, and you know how your children think because you know how they are. And you know how they are because they are just like you.

Things like talents, abilities and musical gifts are also passed down. God taught my mother to play the piano. She never had lessons. When I was thirteen, I sat down at the piano, and the Lord taught me how to play, too. Why? I can't explain it other than to say that I inherited the ability to play the piano from my mother. It was a strength that was passed down to me from her—a gift from the Holy Spirit, passed on to me from Mama. To this day I can play stringed instruments without a single lesson.

In the same way, my wife has always been good at math. Our children are all strong in math skills because their mama (and their daddy, to a certain extent) had strong math skills.

Iniquity: What Is It?

Our weaknesses are also inherited. The Bible calls them *iniquity.*

Take two parents who have hot tempers, for example, and you'll invariably find children who have hot tempers, too. It's amazing how children grow up exhibiting the identical soulish attitudes and traits of their parents. Something will come up that sets them off, and they'll flash. Then, if they're Christians, they'll spend the next two weeks repenting of losing their tempers for five minutes.

Has that ever happened to you? If it has—if you have that same hot temper your daddy had—you've identified iniquity.

What is iniquity? *Iniquity* is an inherited propensity for certain sin. It is the inherent weakness in the soul for a particular sin, or sins, that we all inherit from our fore-fathers.

At a point of repentance for his own transgressions and iniquities, David wrote:

> Behold, I was shapen in iniquity; and in sin did my mother conceive me.
>
> —PSALM 51:5, KJV

Later he addressed the serious nature of unresolved iniquity by writing:

> If I regard iniquity in my heart, the Lord will not hear me: but verily God hath heard me; he hath attended to the voice of my prayer.
>
> —PSALM 66:18–19, KJV

Did you hear that? David said God would not hear the prayers of the man or woman who refused to deal with his or her own iniquities. The person who regards or entertains or attaches himself to iniquity will not have his prayers answered. David also wrote that once iniquity is dealt with, God will once more answer prayer.

According to the Bible, iniquity is formed through repetitive sin. Repetitive transgression produces a weakness or propensity for certain sins. Whether it be character traits present in a person's nature, ungodly attitudes found within the soulish realm or tendencies toward certain sins in the physical realm, these weaknesses—iniquities—are passed down again and again from one generation to the next. They will continue to be passed down until you or someone in your lineage repents before God and gets those iniquities under the blood of Jesus. The Bible says that when a person repents, he will not bear the brunt of the iniquity any longer. (See Ezekiel 18.)

There is deliverance from inherited iniquity. It is possible to walk out from under those undesirable, ungodly ancestral traits that have made you like your ancestors.

> *When you begin to understand what iniquity is, you will be able to recognize it instantly when it rears its ugly head, and you will be able to break its power over you.*

When you begin to understand what iniquity is, you will be able to recognize it instantly when it rears its ugly head, and you will be able to break its power over you. Once you recognize iniquity, by faith you will be able to speak to it and apply the finished work of Calvary to break the power of iniquity over your life. We are going to talk specifically about how to break iniquity in upcoming chapters. When you get hold of this lesson, your entire soul nature will change—your mind, your will, your emotions. You'll find yourself walking in victory for the first time ever. You'll find power to overcome those same old sins that have come up again and again, threatening to take you down. Now, if that's not good news, what is?

Addictive Thoughts

Echoes from the past and sinful behaviors lead to addictive thought patterns. We become addicted to a way of thinking. I believe every person is an "addict" in some way, for better or for worse. I might be able to sing a song from your raucous youth before you met Christ, and you would start thinking about Suzie or Tom or whomever you were with when you heard it—and it may take you days to get it out of your mind. Some people can look at a billboard on the side of the road, and it will set off a chain reaction of visual pictures in the imagination that take weeks and months to get rid of. That's why the world sells sex. Not even chewing gum is marketed any more without the advertisement showing a provocative body. The world knows that people are mentally addicted to different thoughts.

Many people are addicted to thought patterns based on past experience, and these thought patterns are as addictive as a drug. Because of past experience, some people automatically mistrust when they should trust, doubt when they should believe, react negatively when truth is in front of them. They are addicted to thought patterns that produce an automatic behavior.

Simon the Ex-Sorcerer

One of the greatest examples of addictive thought patterns in Scripture is found in Simon the ex-sorcerer, whom we meet in Acts 8. Simon was saved, baptized in water and baptized in the Holy Spirit. He was present to observe the impact that the ministry of the apostles in Jerusalem was having on the people around them.

> And when Simon saw that through the laying on of the apostles' hands the Holy Spirit was given, he offered them money, saying, "Give me this power also, that anyone on whom I lay hands may receive the Holy Spirit."
>
> —ACTS 8:18–19

Simon thought he could buy and control everything through money. Maybe his motive was pure, but his method was sinful. You can't buy, bottle or sell the Holy Spirit.

The same is true of you. Your motive can be right—
you may feel totally justified in what you want or
do—but your method has to line up with the Word of
God. Many Christians, although they have come out of
the world, still try to serve God with carnal motives and
methods. They say, "Well, the end result is that somebody's going to hear the gospel somewhere." But if you
live like hell, talk like hell and act like hell, no one will
ever hear the gospel. God wants your method to change.

What was Peter's answer to Simon? "Your money
perish with you, because you thought that the gift of
God could be purchased with money! You have neither
part nor portion in this matter, for your heart is not right
in the sight of God. Repent therefore..." (vv. 20-22).
Peter looked at Simon the ex-sorcerer and said, "I know
you said yes to Jesus Christ, but that doesn't mean your
thoughts are right. You had better change the way you
think about money."

Simon was a Spirit-filled guy with an unrenewed
mind. He was addicted to a process of thinking about
money. Peter exhorts him, "Repent therefore of this your
wickedness, and pray God if perhaps the thought of
your heart may be forgiven you. For I see . . . " (vv.
22-23). The King James version states, "For I perceive . . . " The Greek word for *perceive* is *horao*, from
which we get our word *horizon*. It means to see a big
picture. For example, the Books of Exodus and Hebrews
both say that when Moses was born his mother and
father looked into his face, and they saw the *horao*, the
big picture that indicated he was no ordinary child.

When God starts setting a person free, that person may
not see the exact way out of the problems that had
bogged him or her down as an unbeliever. Often it takes
another person—someone like Peter was to Simon—to
see the big picture and help that person find the way out.

Peter was saying, "I see the big picture about you,

Simon." Peter told Simon, "I perceive that thou art in the gall of bitterness, and in the bond of iniquity" (v. 23, KJV). The word *bond* in the Greek means "a uniting ligament," like the ligaments in the arm that unite different parts of your hand and your body. Peter says, "You have been united and linked together with that iniquitous thought." The word *iniquity* is the word *adikia*, from which we get our word *addicted.* Peter said, "Simon, I know you are born again, I know you are saved, and I know that you love God. But let me tell you something; you're handling it all wrong. You have an addictive thought pattern. You have a compulsive behavior, and even though Jesus is your Lord, you're still living like hell. You better ask God to get you free from that, or it will destroy you."

Personally, I believe that Simon was freed from his addictive thought because a brother in Christ pointed him in the right direction and taught him how to be free.

Iniquities, Not Demons

It's sad that some people have gone to every sort of preacher there is to get victory over repetitive sin. Some people believe they have a demon every time they sin, and they think they have to go get it cast out. It's one of the saddest errors in present teaching in the body of Christ—that people who are saved and filled with the Holy Spirit can also be demon possessed. They no more have demons than I'm an astronaut. They simply were never delivered from the power of iniquity in their soulish man. The mind, with desires and emotions, comprises the soul of man.

It's not demons that cause so many Christians to be constantly tripped up by repeat sin—it's iniquity.

Have you ever known someone who was an alcoholic?

Perhaps this person had a houseful of children—all of whom made bold statements like, "When I'm grown I'll never take a drink, because I've seen firsthand what alcohol does to people. I saw what it did to Mama (or Daddy), and I'll never drink that stuff." But then when the pressure is on, the kids break their resolve, and nine out of ten of them wind up with an alcohol problem, too. What happened?

Iniquity is what happened. The children inherited the weakness toward the sin of alcoholism from their parent (or parents). How many ancestors before their parents had also demonstrated a weakness toward alcoholism? There is absolutely no telling.

The devil has consistently snared men and women throughout history into the bondage of iniquity. That's how he holds them—by their iniquities. It is common knowledge among the research community that parents who drink will often raise children who drink; parents who abuse their children will often raise children who, as adults, become abusive parents. Research also shows that children who were molested often grow up to become child molesters themselves. Some psychologists today chalk that up to environmental living or association. They say it's all in how a person is raised. But the Bible calls it iniquity.

Suppressing Iniquity Is Not Enough

Some people continually suppress iniquity. But simply denying the existence of iniquity is not the same as receiving deliverance from its power. If you suppress iniquity, it may still crop up later—even more powerfully than if you had stopped along the way to deal with it. That's why some people who used to drink find themselves reverting back to alcohol after many years of sobriety. If they did not receive deliverance from their iniquity, the devil may still attempt to turn their thoughts toward alcohol. He will increase the pressure by degrees until eventually the person returns to drinking. Or perhaps the snare is drugs. Whatever the weakness, you can be certain that the devil will try to find it and apply the pressure. He will keep you in guilt or condemnation because of your mental attraction to your iniquity, even if you are strong enough to keep yourself from acting out your sin.

"Oh, no—I'm a Christian," you say. Yes, even some Christians have to fight a battle to keep from telling lies. Other Christians have a weakness for pornography. They may say, "Oh, I don't want to do that." But they are powerless against its lure and are eventually drawn back into the snare of pornography. That's iniquity. Because they do not understand how to overcome it, they try to suppress it. And if suppressing it is not effective, then they feel it's a hopeless cause, and they simply roll over and submit to it.

> *Simply denying the existence of iniquity is not the same as receiving deliverance from its power.*

How God Dealt With My Own Iniquities

Yes, even that Hallam hot temper is another iniquity. It's the thing God had to deal with me about before I could become a preacher. For thirty years I knew God had a call on my life, but I ran. For thirty years I ran when I could have been preaching the gospel and accomplishing God's purpose for my life. I ran because I had a hot temper. I did not do the will of God. I knew God wanted me to preach. I was raised in East Texas, and every time a Spirit-filled preacher came through town, he laid hands on me and prophesied that God had called me to preach. But I didn't want to preach, and I ran.

The Holy Spirit never let up. He kept saying, "You're not doing what I told you to do. You're not doing what I told you to do." Sometimes I'd get bold and rebuke the voice and say, "What I'm doing must certainly be the will of God for my life because, after all, things are going so good." I had resolved myself to becoming a multimillionaire and a deacon—in that order. That's having pride in iniquity. Many people are never delivered from their iniquities because they have become prideful about their sin. They have given up the battle to be set free because of so many past defeats in that area.

I was in business and didn't want anything to do with full-time ministry, but the Holy Spirit kept bringing it up in my spirit. Finally I couldn't run any more, and I said, "OK, God, if preaching is what You want me to do, I'm ready to serve You. I'll preach the gospel. I'll teach the Word. I don't care what You want me to do—I'll do it. Just open the doors." Even as I prayed, I knew there were certain character traits in me that would have to go— like my hot temper. All of my life, it had caused me trouble. It caused me trouble in high school. It caused me trouble in college. It caused me trouble in the service, on the job, when I took my car to the mechanic, on the highway behind the wheel of the car. It even caused me trouble in church when it was time to deal with my Christian brothers and sisters. How in the world could I preach with a temper like mine? I said, "God, I've got to have some help with this thing."

That's when God began to reveal to me what iniquity was about. He said, "You have iniquity in your life, and you have not dealt with it through the blood of Jesus." He showed me what it was and what to do about it.

After its power over my life was broken, I found it was natural to line up with God's will for my life and start preaching. One day I woke up and said, "All I've got is one life. I can't wait until I become a multimillionaire before I decide to serve God. If I'm going to serve God, I'd better do it now."

I was in Detroit, Michigan, at a conference in 1980 when God broke through to my understanding and revealed to me what iniquity was and how to be set free from it—forever. I left Detroit and headed back to East Texas, and I couldn't wait to get there. When I got home, I went to the bedroom, knelt down beside the bed and said, "God, if You're real, then I know You can deal with every sin in my life." I began to talk to Him personally, and that's when He began to give me insight about iniquity.

Get Honest With God

Sometimes you have to get honest with God. Sometimes everybody else is not the problem—you are the problem. That's what He showed me. He showed me that I was the problem. Not only did I have this hot temper, but I was also jealous. I never had a reason to be jealous, but I was, nevertheless, a jealous man. It was a part of my nature. I said, "God, I can't even stay married to the best woman in the world without fighting every week. And there's no reason to fight."

God had already begun to deal with me in this area of iniquity by showing me that I was the problem. He also showed me that jealousy was something that was in my nature—an iniquity that had been passed down to me. He showed me that Jesus had already been bruised for it. And as I saw the truth, I began to cry out, "Jesus, I believe You have been bruised for my iniquity. I confess this weakness—jealousy—in my life, and I ask that Your power flow into that area to bring deliverance."

As I spoke, fear departed and faith rose up in me. I confessed over and over every day that I was no longer a jealous man with a hot temper. Why? Because Jesus was bruised for those iniquities that had been passed down to me. Can you see it? Those iniquities had been controlling me and limiting my horizons for many years. When God dealt with me about the nature of iniquity, I was able to apply His Word, by faith, to overcome the very things that had been spiritual stumbling blocks.

And do you know what happened? *Victory* is what happened. When faith comes, so does victory.

> When faith comes, so does victory.

Not long after I started pastoring, the Holy Spirit said to me, "If you'll walk upright and obey My Word, no man will ever be able to keep you from doing what I have told you to do." I became a happy preacher right that minute, because I believe God when He speaks. I became perfectly at peace with pastoring—the very thing I ran from for so long. I was happy because God had revealed how to conquer the areas of iniquity in my own life that had been causing me to stumble—causing me to run. I found that I could obey His voice and fulfill that call on my life.

This is a message every preacher needs to get in his spirit. Many preachers who have fallen did so because their own iniquities slew them. It was not because they did not love God. It was because they had areas—weaknesses in their natures, in their minds, their wills, their emotions—that had not been put under the blood of Jesus. These iniquities—passed down to them from their forefathers—eventually rose up and caused their downfall.

The Difference Between Sin and Iniquity

First John, chapter 2, describes *transgression* as the willful breaking of God's law, or the *external* manifestation of sin. A transgression is something that can be seen on the outside. It is sin made manifest. What does the Bible say about sin made manifest? It says that Jesus was wounded for it. "He was wounded for our transgressions" (Isa. 53:5). Calvary took care of sin for you and me. His death on the cross purchased our forgiveness for sins and gave us the power to stand before God, sanctified.

Isaiah 53:5 also says, "He was bruised for our iniquities." A bruise is not something that is always outwardly visible. The worst bruises are internal. When a bruise does become outwardly visible, it is because some type of injury has occurred internally to cause the blood to rise up to the surface of the skin and pool beneath it, causing dark, discolored blotches that are tender to the touch. Jesus was "bruised for our iniquities"—those things that are hidden beneath the surface, those inherent weaknesses that cause us to sin only when they rise up and are acted upon. Calvary, then, covered both our *transgressions* and our *iniquities.* Jesus died for the sins that are outwardly visible, or manifested, as well as those latent, inherent tendencies toward sin that the devil uses to really put the pressure on us.

Let's look at Isaiah 53:5 in its entirety:

> But He was wounded for our transgressions, He was bruised for our iniquities; the chastisement for our peace was upon Him, and by His stripes we are healed.

Jesus paid the price once and for all for our iniquities. There was no other way for mankind to be released from the force of iniquity. Ephesians 2:3 states:

> Among whom also we all once conducted our-
> selves in the lusts of our flesh, fulfilling the desires
> of the flesh and of the mind, and were by nature
> children of wrath, just as the others.

What does that passage of Scripture say? It says we
were by nature the children of wrath. Before what?
Before Calvary.

Before we were born again and filled with the Holy
Spirit, that nature ruled our lives. That nature still remains
in some people even after they are born again. Even
though they are born again, these individuals often do
not live consistent godly lives because they still have
iniquities present in their lives. Romans 5:12 says that
because one man sinned, that same death passed on to
all mankind. We all inherited the iniquitous nature. For
that reason, a person could conceivably live a perfect
life, never commit one sin and still not be found perfect
before God unless he receives Jesus Christ as Savior.

That iniquitous nature, present on the inside even
though dormant, carries the propensity for sin even if sin
has actually never been acted out. That's why none of us
can save ourselves. Each of us needs Jesus. He is the only
One who can deal with both sin and the sin nature.

Thank God for grace!

What Happened at Calvary

At Calvary, Christ took care of all three dimensions of
your being—spirit, soul and body.

He took care of the spiritual realm by making available to you eternal life in the presence of His Father. He
took care of the external, physical realm when He died
for your sins. He was wounded for your transgressions
(Isa. 53:5). A *wound* is external bleeding. *Transgression*
is "the outward, external breaking of God's commands."

Jesus was wounded externally for your transgressions.

He took care of your inner man—your soulish man, which is your will and your emotions. He was bruised for your iniquities. A *bruise* is "internal bleeding and cannot be readily seen outwardly." All those iniquitous urges to sin, driving you toward eventually acting them out, can be brought under the power of the blood of Christ so that your soulish man also experiences the full deliverance promised in the Word of God:

> The chastisement for our peace was upon Him, and by His stripes we are healed. All we like sheep have gone astray; we have turned, every one, to his own way; and the LORD has laid on Him the iniquity of us all. He was oppressed and He was afflicted, yet He opened not His mouth; He was led as a lamb to the slaughter, and as a sheep before its shearers is silent, so He opened not His mouth. He was taken from prison and from judgment, and who will declare His generation? For He was cut off from the land of the living; for the transgressions of My people He was stricken. And they made His grave with the wicked—but with the rich at His death, because He had done no violence, nor was any deceit in His mouth.
>
> Yet it pleased [satisfied] the LORD to bruise Him; He has put Him to grief. When You make His soul an offering for sin, He shall see His seed, He shall prolong His days, and the pleasure of the LORD shall prosper in His hand. He shall see the labor of His soul, and be satisfied. By His knowledge My righteous Servant shall justify many, for He shall bear their iniquities.
>
> —ISAIAH 53:5–11

Jesus was chastised for your peace. If you have iniquity

within you, constantly keeping you in turmoil, that's not peace. There are many people who are saved and filled with the Holy Spirit, yet they have no peace. They walk around in condemnation for their whole lives because they are bound by iniquity.

To illustrate the many subtle shades of iniquity, Jesus said, "Whoever looks at a woman to lust for her has already committed adultery with her in his heart" (Matt. 5:28). Prior to this teaching, it was understood that it was wrong to *commit* adultery. Now Jesus was exposing the hidden man of the heart, revealing that iniquity—not just transgression—was a serious offense to God. The heart is where iniquity is found. And if your heart, bound by iniquity, condemns you, how can you be at peace with God?

Jesus purchased your peace on the cross at Calvary. God does not just want you to be redeemed spiritually. He does not just want a covenant with your flesh. He wants all of you—spirit, flesh, mind, will, emotions—and the finished work of Christ upon the cross has purchased that for you. He will empower you by subduing those iniquities that have caused you so much trouble. He will cast your sin into the sea and subdue your iniquities. That's powerful!

Far too often we claim the legal experiences that belong to us in Christ Jesus but never experience the manifestations of what legally has been purchased for us in Christ Jesus. The Bible says that Christ has redeemed us from the curse of the law (Gal. 3:13). The word *redeemed* is a beautiful word in the Greek. It's the word *exagorazo*. We get our word *exaggerate* from it. It literally means "an excessive amount" or "more than necessary."

I contend that one drop of Jesus' blood would have redeemed all of humanity, because the only thing divine on this planet when Jesus walked with us was the blood inside His body. Everything else was carnal. He could have used one drop of blood to totally anesthetize all of humanity's problems, which Adam loosed on earth. By the shedding of blood, there was the removal of the wages of sin and the effects of sin. But the Bible says that Christ redeemed us by paying an excessive, exaggerated price to redeem us from all the curses of hell. I get pretty excited when I think about that.

I'm reminded of a story—no doubt fictional—set in a slave auction back when the United States was still involved in the slave trade. Prospective buyers were walking around in their expensive clothes looking at the slaves, inspecting them, being condescending and speaking negatively about them. They wanted to humiliate the slaves a little bit before they actually bought them, and they wanted to point out any defects so they could get them for a better price.

I contend that one drop of Jesus' blood would have redeemed all of humanity.

One of the slaves to be auctioned was a little lady who was crippled and broken down; she had sustained several maladies from traveling on the slave ship. As she came up to the auction block for sale, someone called out, "I'll bid ten dollars." Everybody laughed. Someone else said, "I'll bid eleven dollars." Everybody laughed again. The woman slouched and tried to hide her face as she went through the humiliation.

But someone stepped out of the crowd and cried out, "I'll bid one thousand dollars." Everyone gasped. The person, who looked like someone of high rank and nobility, walked up to the auction block. When no more bids came in, the auctioneer said, "Sold." The nobleman went up to the slave woman, took her arm and walked her like a bride through the crowd in front of everybody. Then he announced in the hearing of everyone, "I have bought you and paid a price that no one else could outbid—just so I can let you go." Turning to the crowd, he said, "I'm telling everybody publicly...she belongs to me, and I release her. If you give her any trouble, you'll have to deal with me."

That man demonstrated the meaning of the word *exagorazo*.

Just like that slave woman, humanity was taken into captivity through the sin of Adam and Eve. The rest of us had nothing to do with it. We didn't earn the curse. We didn't deserve it. Yet Christ paid an exaggerated amount for my freedom—and for yours. He bought you. You've become His bride, and He has released you to live free of iniquity. If hell messes with you, it will have to deal with Him.

Chapter 6

Overcoming Iniquity

WITHOUT JESUS, THERE would be no grace available to sinners. Before He came to pay the ultimate penalty for mankind's sin, there was one way a person could hope for heaven—by keeping the Law. Funny thing about keeping the Law—a person had to keep the whole Law, or none of it would be of any use. Either keep all the Ten Commandments or nullify the ones a person found he could not keep effectively. God's standard was—is, and has always been—100 percent perfection. Only Jesus—perfectly man, totally God—could meet that impossibly high standard.

Practically every iniquity committed by men can be identified in one of the Ten Commandments. Once that sin has begun in a person's life, if he does not repent of it and turn away from it, it will develop into an internal character trait. This trait can be passed inherently to the offspring in the nature or soul. Thus it becomes an iniquity—a genetic weakness or "birth defect" in the nature of a man for a particular sin.

What the Bible Says About Iniquity

I believe that each commandment was God's way of trying to deal with major iniquity in mankind. Thus the Ten Commandments were given by God, not to keep people from having fun, but to keep them alive until the only One who could break humanity's iniquity—the Messiah, Jesus Christ—would come and deliver us from our sins.

By simply studying and being aware of the moral and spiritual failures of the world around us today, we can easily describe the iniquity that corresponds to each commandment. Here is a list of the Ten Commandments found in Exodus 20 and the iniquities that each commandment was given to prevent.

1. "Thou shalt have no other gods before me" (v. 3, KJV). Iniquities covered: Rebellion, witchcraft, occult, New Age.

2. "Thou shalt not make unto thee any graven image, or any likeness of any thing that is in heaven above, or that is in the earth beneath, or that is in the water under the earth: thou shalt not bow down thyself to them, nor serve them" (vv. 4–5, KJV). Iniquities covered: Idolatry, stubbornness, rebellion.

3. "Thou shalt not take the name of the LORD thy God in vain; for the LORD will not hold him guiltless that taketh his name in vain" (v. 7, KJV). Iniquities covered: Cursing, filthy talk, speaking death instead of life.

4. "Remember the sabbath day, to keep it holy. Six days shalt thou labour, and do all thy work: but

the seventh day is the sabbath of the L ORD thy God; in it thou shalt not do any work, thou, nor thy son, nor thy daughter, thy manservant, nor thy maidservant, nor thy cattle, nor thy stranger that is within thy gates: for in six days the L ORD made heaven and earth, the sea, and all that in them is, and rested the seventh day: wherefore the L ORD blessed the sabbath day, and hallowed it" (vv. 8–11, KJV). Iniquities covered: No peace of mind, no rest, discontentment, nervousness, family quarrels, suicides.

5. "Honour thy father and thy mother: that thy days may be long upon the land which the L ORD thy God giveth thee" (v. 12, KJV). Iniquities covered: Disobedience, rebellion, premature death, depression, crime, tempers, depression.

6. "Thou shalt not kill" (v. 13, KJV). Iniquities covered: Murder, violent crime, hate.

7. "Thou shalt not commit adultery" (v. 14, KJV). Iniquities covered: Sexual uncleanness, venereal diseases, divorces, unfaithfulness, jealousy, suspicion, homosexuality.

8. "Thou shalt not steal" (v. 15, KJV). Iniquities covered: Stealing, robbery, greed.

9. "Thou shalt not bear false witness against thy neighbour" (v. 16, KJV). Iniquities covered: Lying, dishonesty, deception, mistrust.

10. "Thou shalt not covet thy neighbour's house, thou shalt not covet thy neighbour's wife, nor his manservant, nor his maidservant, nor his ox, nor

his ass, nor any thing that is thy neighbour's" (v. 17, KJV). Iniquities covered: Jealousy, strife, envy, greed.

The list of most heinous sins is not long, yet throughout history mankind has found it next to impossible to keep all of the commandments. These commandments, if kept, can retard the growth of ten major groups of iniquities in human nature. These iniquities are a compounded by-product of Adam's fall, and they have been passed on to all mankind.

This chapter of Exodus, which has so much to say on the subject of sin, also includes the subject of iniquity.

> I, the LORD your God, am a jealous God, visiting the iniquity of the fathers upon the children to the third and fourth generations of those who hate Me; but showing mercy to thousands, to those who love Me and keep My commandments.
>
> —EXODUS 20:5–6

Remember, *iniquity* is "the propensity or weakness for sin, passed down from one generation to the next." A father caught in the habitual, repetitive sin of alcoholism passes down that weakness for alcohol to his children. And that weakness—that iniquity—will keep right on being passed down until someone takes authority over it and, by faith, applies the atoning blood of Jesus to it to break its power in their lives. Then not only will the power of iniquity be broken in their own lives, but it will also be broken over the generations to come.

Even in the Old Testament, God was addressing the issue of deliverance from mankind's sin. All iniquity stems from the breaking of God's commandments. In the Book of Numbers, God grew tired of continually dealing with the rebellious Israelites. When the Lord told Moses He intended to kill them all, Moses rose to their defense:

Now if thou shalt kill all this people as one man, then the nations which have heard the fame of thee will speak, saying, Because the LORD was not able to bring this people into the land which he sware unto them, therefore he hath slain them in the wilderness. And now, I beseech thee, let the power of my Lord be great, according as thou hast spoken, saying, The LORD is longsuffering, and of great mercy, forgiving iniquity and transgression, and by no means clearing the guilty, visiting the iniquity of the fathers upon the children unto the third and fourth generation. Pardon, I beseech thee, the iniquity of this people according unto the greatness of thy mercy, and as thou hast forgiven this people, from Egypt even until now. And the LORD said, I have pardoned according to thy word.

—NUMBERS 14:15–20, KJV

Moved by the intercession of Moses on behalf of the Israelites, the Lord spared them and gave us a glimpse of the Deliverer to come—Jesus—who was bruised at Calvary, ensuring our victory over iniquity in this dispensation.

Our Merciful God

One of the greatest things I can teach you is *who Christ is to you* and *who you are in Christ.* Once you get that in your spirit, you will be new in your spirit, new in your flesh and new in your inner man—your soul.

You'll no longer have trouble getting a renewed mind because you'll have brand-new thought patterns, brand-new desires, brand-new ambitions, brand-new goals and brand-new dreams, and they'll be pleasing to God—no longer things of the flesh. (See Ephesians 4:23; Philippians 2:5.)

You may actually believe there is no hope. You know how you are on the inside. You know the way you think, what you secretly long for and how you continually struggle with the temptation to sin. To you, I say it is by the mercy of God that you are reading this book, because once you get hold of this message, you'll be set free.

> The LORD . . . keeping mercy for thousands, forgiving iniquity and transgression and sin, by no means clearing the guilty, visiting the iniquity of the fathers upon the children and the children's children to the third and the fourth generation.
>
> —EXODUS 34:6–7

Do you see how these iniquities—these weaknesses that drive you to sin in certain areas—are passed down? It is by God's mercy that you can be free of those iniquities.

Proverbs 26:2 states, "Like a flitting sparrow, like a flying swallow, so a curse without cause shall not alight." Now, that's an interesting passage of scripture. In essence, this verse is asserting that there's something internal—some hidden reason—why any curse attaches itself to you. If you have been walking around in a daze, feeling as though half of the things you do are cursed, yet you can't think of anything you did to cause it—*something* caused it. "A curse without cause shall not alight." There's something behind it, driving it. You may say, "Well, I haven't robbed anybody. I haven't killed anyone. I haven't lied."

Quit blaming God for your misfortune. Get into the Word, find out where you may have missed God. Proverbs 26:27 states, "Whoever digs a pit will fall into it, and he who rolls a stone will have it roll back on him." It may have been some internal, hidden stone that you rolled, but eventually every stone will roll back upon you—it will catch up to you. But I have good news for you. Even when it appears that every time you try to rise up you fall back down again, there is hope. Even if you have to start all over again from square one, there is hope.

> Do not rejoice over me, my enemy; when I fall, I will arise; when I sit in darkness, the LORD will be a light to me....He will bring me forth to the light; I will see His righteousness.
>
> —MICAH 7:8–9

Perhaps you have been sitting in darkness. Perhaps it looks as if there is no way out. Your merciful God has made a way of escape for you.

> Blessed be the LORD, who has not given us as prey to their teeth. Our soul has escaped as a bird from the snare of the fowlers; the snare is broken, and we have escaped. Our help is in the name of the LORD, who made heaven and earth.
>
> —PSALM 124:6–8

There is a way of escape. There is a way back up. "When I fall, I will arise" (Mic. 7:8). "Now thanks be to God who always leads us in triumph in Christ" (2 Cor. 2:14). Even if you fall seven times, He'll pick you up.

You need to start reminding the devil of that. Start saying, "Listen, Devil, don't mess with me. You may trip me up today, but in the name of Jesus

Even when it appears that every time you try to rise up you fall back down again, there is hope.

Christ, if I fall seven times, I'll get back up again. He'll help me."

A righteous man will always get back up. That doesn't mean he wasn't guilty of sinning. It means that he's going to get back up because of what Jesus did for him at Calvary. Iniquity may trip up a righteous man, but it doesn't have to keep him down. And when he falls, he can rise up again. A righteous man will get back up because Jesus was bruised for his iniquities. The mercy of God will maintain him until he can get the full benefit of the victory purchased by Jesus on the cross, at Calvary.

> Who is a God like You, pardoning iniquity and passing over the transgression of the remnant of His heritage? He does not retain His anger forever, because He delights in mercy. He will again have compassion on us, and will subdue our iniquities. You will cast all our sins into the depths of the sea.
>
> —MICAH 7:18–19

The Old Testament prophet Micah was prophesying of the day when Christ would atone for the sum of mankind's sins. At the time this passage of text was written, Israel was trapped in its own iniquity with no way out except to keep all of the Law. Micah was prophesying of the New Covenant—a time when men could meet God face to face with their sins covered in the blood of Jesus. Even when the Law was kept, the Israelites could not hope for deliverance from iniquity. Their sacrifices could only cover them from year to year while they waited for the promised Messiah.

Today Christ's blood covers not just the sins of a single year, but the sum of all your sins. Thank God, He will also subdue your iniquity.

How to Deal Effectively With Iniquity

Dealing with the flesh is nothing new. The apostle Paul wrestled with his flesh, as did others who were powerfully used by God to turn the world upside down. Paul wrote:

> For I know that in me (that is, in my flesh) nothing good dwells; for to will is present with me, but how to perform what is good I do not find. For the good that I will to do, I do not do; but the evil I will not to do, that I practice. Now if I do what I will not to do, it is no longer I who do it, but sin that dwells in me. I find then a law, that evil is present with me, the one who wills to do good. For I delight in the law of God according to the inward man. But I see another law in my members, warring against the law of my mind, and bringing me into captivity to the law of sin which is in my members. O wretched man that I am! Who will deliver me from this body of death? I thank God—through Jesus Christ our Lord.
>
> —ROMANS 7:18–25

Paul knew that Jesus was—and is—the way out of the internal struggle of sin and iniquity. He is the way. He doesn't want you to have some little spiritual experience and then revert back to all those old habits and fallen thinking processes. He wants your mind to be renewed. (See Ephesians 4:23.) And you can't have a renewed mind until you learn how to get

> *Jesus was—and is—the way out of the internal struggle of sin and iniquity. He is the way.*

free from iniquity—those inherent weaknesses in the soul (mind) prompting you to sin.

Later, in 2 Timothy 2:24–26, Paul wrote:

> And a servant of the Lord must not quarrel but be gentle to all, able to teach, patient, in humility correcting those who are in opposition, if God perhaps will grant them repentance, so that they may know the truth, and that they may come to their senses and escape the snare of the devil, having been taken captive by him to do his will.

Have you ever met someone like that—someone who always opposes himself, who is his own worst enemy? With his mouth he says, "I love God," and even with his works he shows his love for God. But he keeps opposing himself internally. That's iniquity. The Bible says we pastors are to instruct those who oppose themselves, pointing the way toward deliverance.

How do you receive deliverance from the power of iniquity? First, by acknowledging the truth, then by repentance. Don't be too proud to admit the truth. God knows it, and you know it. Now it's time to admit it before God in prayer. Then you can be set free from it.

In the remainder of this book we will address walking out the process of deliverance.

No One Is Without Iniquity

I have never known anyone who did not have some iniquity somewhere in his or her life. Without a revelation of the power of Jesus Christ, that iniquity will get bigger inside you the older you get. But if you realize this simple revelation, God will set you free. You won't spend all of your life repenting over transgressions, because that thing called *iniquity* that was pressing you to transgress will have been properly dealt with. You will no longer bring to fruition the work of iniquity on the inside of you. God will change you on the inside. He will even change your emotions. No longer will you oppose yourself, because the iniquity that was driving you will have been subdued.

Deliverance from the power of iniquity is promised in the Word of God. Jeremiah prophesied it would be so:

> In those days they shall say no more: "The fathers have eaten sour grapes, and the children's teeth are set on edge." But every one shall die for his own iniquity; every man who eats the sour grapes, his teeth shall be set on edge. Behold, the days are coming, says the LORD, when I will make a new covenant with the house of Israel and with the house of Judah—not according to the covenant that I made with their fathers in the day that I took them by the hand to lead them out of the land of Egypt, My covenant which they broke, though I was a husband to them, says the LORD. But this is the covenant that I will make with the house of Israel after those days, says the LORD: I will put My law in their minds, and write it on their hearts; and I will be their God, and they shall be My people. No more shall every man teach his neighbor, and every man his brother, saying, "Know the LORD," . . . for I will forgive their iniquity, and their sin I will remember no more.
>
> —JEREMIAH 31:29–34

Jesus was the fulfillment of Jeremiah's prophecy. He purchased our freedom from both sin and iniquity. Yet it continually amazes me how some Christians will try to "segmentize" what Jesus did on Calvary. They say, "Oh, I believe Jesus is the Son of God. I believe He died on

Calvary and rose on the third day." They may even say, "I believe Jesus was wounded for my transgressions—my sins. Jesus, save me." And Jesus will forgive them. But what about their iniquities? If they don't move on into a revelation of the total work of Christ on Calvary, they will continue in their iniquities and pass them on to their children.

> *There was not one wasted stripe, torment or form of torture endured by our Savior. He paid the full penalty—spiritual, soulful, physical and mental—to redeem humanity.*

Remember, a wound is external, like a transgression, but a bruise is internal, like iniquity. Jesus was bruised for our iniquities. Yet some people never take time to understand what that means. Consequently, they lump transgression and iniquity together and never get the full benefit of Calvary. By the same token, there are some who do not grasp the full revelation of what the Scripture means when it states, "By His stripes you are healed." These individuals may die prematurely and may suffer all kinds of diseases. Does this mean that God's Word isn't true? No, it simply means these individuals lacked revelation knowledge of God's promises to heal.

There was not one wasted stripe, torment or form of torture endured by our Savior. He paid the full penalty—spiritual, soulful, physical and mental—to redeem humanity. He was bruised for your iniquities. When the revelation of that begins to come alive in your spirit, you will be able to say, "I see it now."

94

Redeemed From the Curse of the Law

The Law was weak. Far from perfect, the Law was meant to expose human weakness—not to uphold human strengths. This means that a person who is born again may be able to abstain completely from transgression through self-discipline, good moral living and by upholding the standards of goodness and niceness set forth in the Word of God. But the person can still be filled with iniquity. The problem is not external—it's internal. That sin nature passed down to that person from Adam is still right there, seething beneath the surface.

In Galatians, chapter 3, Paul wrote, "But that no one is justified by the law in the sight of God is evident, for 'the just shall live by faith.' . . . Christ has redeemed us from the curse of the law" (vv. 11, 13). Let me give you "Hallam's translation" of what that means. It means, "Christ has redeemed us from the weakness of the Law." The Law was weak. It had no power to justify man nor to redeem him. Christ was the Redeemer required by God for mankind as the perfect sin offering. Regardless of how upright men were apart from Christ, the keeping of the Law was not enough. Paul had been a Pharisee, a Jewish leader who had kept the Law all his life, but not even Paul's observance of the many Jewish laws could purchase for him the redemption he received when he made Christ Lord and Savior.

Christ has redeemed us from weakness—from the weakness of poverty, the weakness of sickness, the weakness of spiritual death. Only His grace makes it possible to overcome the Law and all its weakness.

God's ways are higher than our ways. His thoughts are higher than our thoughts (Isa. 55:9). His grace is greater than anything we can comprehend. It's what kept David alive when he fell before the altar in repentance—an action that by rights should have killed him, since no man had yet touched the glory of God's altar and lived. But David had a revelation of the grace of God. He approached the very presence of God's glory—the ark of the covenant. He touched the altar and lived. God's grace is more powerful than the Law. There is no Law when someone is under grace. It is the goodness of God extended to man.

> **God's grace is more powerful than the Law.**

All it takes to sink this into your spirit is a revelation of Calvary and all Christ did for you there. It's what happened to me when God began to deal with me on the subject of iniquity. I did as Paul admonished in 2 Timothy 2:25-26—I got very honest with God. I acknowledged the truth—no more denial. I said, "God, it's time to get out of denial. It's time to get out of those false feelings and hypocrisy. God, line me up for the move of God that You've planned for me. I will no longer be subdued by my iniquities, because You were bruised for my iniquities." And just like that, my life started to change. I was able to say, as Paul did in 2 Corinthians 2:14, "Now thanks be to God who always leads us in triumph." It can be that way for you, too. "For when I am weak, then I am strong" (2 Cor. 12:10).

If you will get honest with God, stop making excuses, get out of denial and get a revelation of this message, your iniquities will go under the blood of Jesus, and you will be free to renew your mind in the Word of God.

The Man by the Pool at Bethesda

Consider the story of the man who lay by the pool at

Bethesda, crippled by his infirmity. From ancient days, it was said that from time to time angels would appear at the pool of Bethesda and go down into the waters, troubling them. When the waters were troubled, those who first dipped in the pool were said to receive miraculous healings. Many crippled, blind and infirm people were always crowded around the pool at Bethesda, waiting for the angels to trouble the waters.

> Now a certain man was there who had an infirmity thirty-eight years. When Jesus saw him lying there, and knew that he already had been in that condition a long time, He said to him, "Do you want to be made well?" The sick man answered Him, "Sir, I have no man to put me into the pool when the water is stirred up; but while I am coming, another steps down before me." Jesus said to him, "Rise, take up your bed and walk." And immediately the man was made well, took up his bed, and walked.
>
> —JOHN 5:5–9

I can see this guy. He's lying there by the pool, totally powerless to help himself. He's been there off and on for thirty-eight years. Sometimes passersby stopped and gave him a little money. Perhaps they even fed him. But let's be honest: This guy may not have wanted to get down into that pool as badly as he said. He could lay right there in the same condition and get fat off his infirmities. He could sit right there and collect a little money, collect a little sympathy and collect a little food while everybody contributing to his cause had to balance their checkbooks, send their kids off to college and all the rest.

Have you ever known anyone who seemed to be getting fat off his or her problems? I have met some people who are masters at telling their problems. I mean, some people can really work you over with their problems. And they're sincere. But Jesus offers a way of deliverance. I've discovered that if you don't want your problem, you don't have to have it.

You've met people who are constantly talking about their arthritis, their heart condition, their this, their that. I like the way Jesus dealt with problems. He rebuked them! He never said, "My, my, that little heart problem is so sweet. Just live with it a while and suffer. It'll do you good. It'll keep you humble." No, He never had that attitude.

Jesus asked the lame man, "Do you want to be made well?" Then He told him not to sin anymore, or a worse thing would come upon him. What kind of sin could a paralyzed man do? He couldn't rob banks, rape or steal. His sin had to be his iniquities—his internal sins.

What Jesus Didn't Say

Jesus did not say the lame man by the pool at Bethesda was lame because he was born to suffer. Consider the story of the blind man as told in John, chapter 9. In this passage of text, Jesus and the disciples encountered a man who had been blind from birth. The disciples asked Jesus, "Rabbi, who sinned, this man or his parents, that he was born blind?" (John 9:2). Jesus answered, "Neither this man nor his parents sinned, but that the works of God should be revealed in him" (v. 3).

Now, a lot of people interpret that scripture the wrong way. Some believe the man's sole purpose in life was to be healed by Jesus, but God never gave birth defects to anyone simply so that person could eventually be healed. If that were the case, everyone with a birth defect would have to receive healing. I believe some people use this interpretation as a crutch to explain why some individuals are born with birth defects. It's part of the blindness the devil continues to perpetrate on planet earth.

The devil is good at perpetrating blindness. He'll blind you to the truth by telling you that the thing you did fifteen years ago, before you were born again, was so bad that you're still having to pay for it. He'll tell you that a hand laid is a hand played. He'll tell you that what you sowed, you'll have to reap. *But what about sowing some repentance?*
Reap mercy.

The Lord has shown me that He will make null and void the works of unrighteousness in your life if you will sow yourself to righteousness in His kingdom. If you will do that, you will soon see that the fruit you now produce will totally overcome the works of darkness in your past. No one has to be controlled by his past. If you are a Christian, you should only be controlled

> *The Lord has shown me that He will make null and void the works of unrighteousness in your life if you will sow yourself to righteousness in His kingdom.*

by your future—a glorious one. So stop looking behind you at the past, and start looking ahead.

No more excuses. No more denial. It's time to get honest with God . . . time to identify those weaknesses—those iniquities—and lift them before God in prayer. It's time to receive your deliverance. As Jesus asked the man by the pool at Bethesda, "Do you want to be made well?"

Chapter 7

The Process

LIVING BEYOND YESTERDAY is a process. Over-coming iniquity is a process, and this process requires us to change. Change is one of the great ministries of the Holy Spirit—as much a ministry as healing or revelation knowledge. God changes everything progressively into His image, and He's constantly changing you and me into His image. Second Corinthians says we change "from glory to glory, just as by the Spirit of the Lord" (2 Cor. 3:18). Here's some good news: He will never change you backward; He will always change you forward and upward, just as the Greek word *metamorphoo* implies. Metamorphosis is the process of going from one stage to the next. The more you change into His image, the more you can be like Him.

Have you noticed that when you refuse to change, you become stagnant in your spirit? At times it may seem that God has stopped speaking to you, but the problem is your unwillingness to change. God can only speak to you as much as you are willing to change, and He cannot use you any more than you are willing to change.

One of the most necessary keys to change is that you have to desire to change. Simply learning is not changing. You can teach a bank robber good things about finances, but all you've done is make a high-class bank robber out of him. Learning didn't change him. It just helped him learn how to rob banks better.

> *God changes every-thing progressively into His image, and He's constantly changing you and me into His image.*

Learning is not changing. Changing comes from an intense desire to be different. Take, for example, people who have a problem with speeding. They say things like this: "I really shouldn't drive that fast." But for all of their lives, their foot is fighting the gas pedal. They feel convicted for driving eighty-five miles per hour in a sixty-five-mile-per-hour zone, but they don't have the heart to change. You know you are one of those people if your blood runs cold every time you see a policeman—even when you are obeying the law. Why? Because something inside of you knows that your heart is not reformed; only your foot is.

But when a desire to change comes from inside of you, you'll begin to change from the inside out. You won't want to drive eighty-five miles per hour because it's against the law, and you are a law-abiding person. You won't want to waste gas and tear up your car. You won't want to endanger other people. Rather than fighting that gas pedal and feeling guilty, you will restrain yourself and feel terrific about it.

102

Desire to Change

Look at it a different way. Many husbands and wives get along only because they are supposed to get along. When your anniversary rolls around, you buy your husband or wife an anniversary present—a dozen roses, a broach and dinner for your wife, and a nice card for your husband—because that's what you are supposed to do. But there is no joy there. There is no desire. Sadly, that's the way many people live. But there is another way, a way where you desire to bless your mate. You say, "Hallelujah, six more months until our anniversary, and I get to buy my wife some roses and a ring. I love to make her happy and watch her face light up." There's a big difference between "I have to" and "I get to."

One of the most necessary ingredients of change in your life is desire. You have to desire desperately to be conformed to the image of the Lord Jesus, or you will be ruled by your carnality. I've been in counseling sessions with various people that I knew by talking to them they were wasting their time and mine. They didn't want to change. They were just trying to prove who was right or wrong. They were not desiring desperately to find the solution—they were desperately desiring justification.

When you were saved, you had a desire to know Jesus, to be washed in His blood and cleansed of all unrighteousness. We come to the Lord not out of cold calculation, but out of passionate desire to know Him and be like Him. That same desire must be rekindled again and again as we walk out the process of salvation and renewing our minds. I know, legally speaking, that when we were born again, we got the whole package—salvation, forgiveness, healing and so on. I am not diminishing that at all.

Yet a foundational principle of life is that we must walk out the process of salvation experientially. We aren't saved and immediately taken up to heaven. Rather, God spends our lives working on our souls and flesh until we are more like Him at the end than we were at the beginning. Some people want to go to the altar and experience a change that totally eradicates their iniquity and renews their mind instantly. Then when they go home, nothing more needs to be done, and they can live like that until Jesus comes.

But that's not how it works. Colossians 1:13 says that we were translated, or delivered, out of darkness and into the kingdom of His Son. But that's not how it is with our minds. The Bible does not say that we are to be translated by the renewing of the mind; it says that we are to be transformed. Transformation is a process. Translation is instantaneous.

The moment we went from serving the devil to serving the Lord, our spirits were re-created. When you were born again and filled with the Holy Spirit, your spirit was born again and filled with the nature, or the very person, of God. He gave you a measure of His Spirit, a first fruit or a down payment of what is going to come one day. But have you noticed that your body was not born again? The aging process did not start going in reverse when you were born again. Similarly, our soul, or mind, was not changed at salvation. That literally is the balance point of serving God.

When Cindy and I were married more than two decades ago, the covenant was established the moment we each said, "I do." Instantly, we went from being single to being one flesh. But because we were two different people, we discovered that we had to grow into the marriage relationship, so we began to be transformed.

You cannot be transformed just by coming to church. You cannot be transformed just by tithing. You cannot be transformed just by the gifts of the Spirit. You cannot be transformed just by the glorious manifestations of the Holy Spirit. Transformation, the renewing of the mind, comes one choice at a time, one day at a time, one decision to live for Christ at a time—not for the echoes. The desire for deliverance without process is fantasy.

Some of you are ready to get a new set of desires. You want to be like other people who are flowing in the Holy Spirit. You want to get an image of yourself as an overcomer, not a defeated person. You want to think and see yourself released and set free from the bondages of the past. As you take each step, the next step will come easier. Before long, like King David, you will hate iniquity and love righteousness. Change in you will be complete in the areas of life that used to be so difficult.

> *The desire for deliverance without process is fantasy.*

Joy

We must be willing to go through the process of renewing our minds and growing in grace, or we will not be delivered—it's as simple as that. If anybody tells you otherwise, they are not being honest. You see, even Jesus went through a process while here on earth. No, His mind did not need to be renewed, and He had no iniquity to get rid of. But the Bible still says He went through a process to become who He was. In these next few pages I want to explore this idea of the process of renewal in Jesus.

The fact that Jesus was both God and man is a great mystery. He contained the fullness of deity in Himself. He came in human form, but was God in flesh—the very Son of God. The second chapter of Luke says that Jesus "grew." In the footnotes of some Bibles, it will even say that He "developed." I take this second chapter of Luke, and a number of other passages in the Bible, to mean that Jesus went through a process and grew to the point where He could contain the fullness of God in His body.

What the process that took Jesus to a position where He could bodily contain the fullness of the Godhead? Most of us aren't even close. If the fullness of the Godhead got in me, I would probably explode. If Jesus was the perfect ten, and I can develop up to a two by the end of my life, I'll be thrilled. But the Bible clearly tells us that Jesus "grew." How did He grow?

First, He "grew and became strong in spirit" (Luke 2:40). I believe that speaks of joy. The Bible says, "The joy of the Lord is your strength" (Neh. 8:10). Joy is the strength of our inner man, just as Paul says, "To be strengthened with might through His Spirit in the inner man" (Eph. 3:16). Why is joy important? Because it keeps us strong in the face of adversity. The Book of Hebrews tells us that Jesus "who for the joy that was set before Him endured the cross" (Heb. 12:2). This joy overrode the harsh reality that had been presented to Him and which He accepted—to bear the cross for humanity's sake. Joy kept Him strong. He let nothing steal His joy. But He had to grow into that place.

Wisdom

Jesus was also "filled with wisdom" (Luke 2:40). Wisdom and knowledge are two different things. Wisdom is not knowing lots of facts; it's knowing what is right and wrong and good and beneficial in God's eyes. You might be the next Einstein and yet have very little wisdom. Wisdom can only be developed through the process of living and listening to the Holy Spirit, from whom wisdom comes.

One reason we ought to pray in tongues is because "he that speaketh in an unknown tongue speaketh not unto men, but unto God: for no man understandeth him; howbeit in the spirit he speaketh mysteries" (1 Cor. 14:2, KJV). The latter part of this verse in the Amplified Bible says, "He utters secret truths and hidden things [not obvious to the understanding]." Proverbs says that God "stores up sound wisdom for the upright . . . happy is the man who finds wisdom" (Prov. 2:7; 3:13). As you begin to pray in the Spirit, you're speaking the stored-up wisdom of God. God stores it up inside of the clay pot that is your body and soul, and at the right moment He will say, "Draw out now, and your water will have turned to wine." Suddenly what you have prayed in the Spirit has turned into wisdom, whether you knew it was happening or not. God will fill you with wisdom as He filled Jesus with wisdom.

Becoming wise in God's sight ought to be on the top of every Christian's agenda. Proverbs says, "Wisdom is the principal thing; therefore get wisdom" (4:7). If the Bible says that Jesus was filled with wisdom even at that young age, how much more do we need it? Wisdom is a precious commodity, as precious as anything on earth. When you study the Book of Proverbs and the rest of the Bible, you are studying the wisdom of God that, in time, was manifested in the Word made flesh—our Lord Jesus. It may be difficult to understand, but all the wisdom that the Holy Spirit breathed into our sacred writings was eventually embodied in one Person. Reading the Word, then, also helps us in our own process of developing wisdom.

Favor

Luke also tells us that "the grace of God was upon Him" (Luke 2:40). The word *grace* can also be translated "favor." This scripture tells us that Jesus developed the art of walking in the favor of God, in the wisdom of God and in the joy in His Spirit. Because of that, He grew His humanity to the place where He contained, Paul said, the fullness of the Godhead bodily.

None of the rest of us will ever be able to do that while in this life. Paul knew he needed more growth; he said, "Not that I have already attained, or am already perfected; but I . . . press toward the goal for the prize" (Phil. 3:12, 14). None of us should get any ideas that we can *become* Jesus, because we can't. But we should be following in the same process that Jesus went through, because He showed us how to live. Like Him, we should grow.

What does it mean to grow? It means we change from day to day in a direction toward God. In modern terms, we might say we are constantly being up-graded, but it takes work. People who want to grow in God's favor, wisdom and joy need to keep inviting godly counsel into their lives through books, tapes, seminars, sermons, godly music, godly friends and so on. We need to keep qualifying for the next level. We need to show that we can handle the next stage of growth.

> *What does it mean to grow? It means we change from day to day in a direction toward God.*

What if, as children, our bodies kept growing even when our bones were not ready for the extra weight? We would damage and maybe even break them.

What if the stock boy at the grocery store was selected to be president of the company? In all likelihood, the company would crumble.

108

Succeeding in business is the same way. A lot of people want to make a lot of money. But unless they have qualified and grown and gone through a process to become able to handle the new level of responsibility, the devil would take that money right back from them. God will not move you into a level of position or responsibility that you are unprepared to manage.

The same principle applies to your walk with God. You must constantly "grow" into the things with which God is blessing you. If you fail to grow, you have devalued the process necessary to obtain God's blessings, and you will disqualify yourself from moving to the next level.

Making Right Choices

How do we participate in this process of becoming more like Jesus? What is our role? What does God ask us to do?

The way we do it is by making choices. Man is the only thing God created with the power of choice. Everything else on the planet operates on instinct. Every animal God made has the ability of instinct, but man, who was made in the likeness of God, was given the power of choice. Adam and Eve had the power to choose; none of the other animals in the Garden did.

One of the prime anointings of the Lord in a Christian's life is the ability to make right choices. Yet many men and women do not activate this anointing. They fail to make right choices, or they avoid making choices altogether. Every change involves a choice. To fail to make good choices is to fail to grow. I believe that Christians can make right choices with the power and guidance of the Holy Spirit. Let's look at this more closely.

The Bible says that when Jesus was on earth, He had a unique anointing to make the right choice:

Therefore the Lord Himself will give you a sign: Behold, the virgin shall conceive and bear a Son, and shall call His name Immanuel. Curds and honey He shall eat, that He may know to refuse the evil and choose the good. For before the Child shall know to refuse the evil and choose the good, the land that you dread will be forsaken by both her kings.

—ISAIAH 7:14–16

It was prophesied that Jesus would have an anointing to refuse evil and choose good. Somebody once said that we make choices, then choices make us. You are the sum total today of the choices that you have made in life. Like me, you have chosen good things, and you have chosen bad things. But there is an anointing to refuse the evil and chose the good, and that's the anointing we want working in our lives.

> *Every change involves a choice. To fail to make good choices is to fail to grow.*

I don't like the doctrine that you win a few and lose a few. I don't see that in Scripture. There are some great thinkers who will debate me on that point, saying we should placidly go through life winning a few and losing a few, but I do not see that as the plan of God for the body of Christ. Granted, we don't live in a perfect world, and we are not perfect people yet, but just because we haven't come into the fullness of what God has for us doesn't mean we should pull God down to our level of expectation. God is interested in failures—like you and me—but not in failing, thank the Lord. Jesus was not anointed to fail.

He was not anointed to win a few and lose a few. He was not anointed to be deceived sometimes and not be deceived other times. He was anointed to refuse evil and choose good.

Jesus was anointed to make the right choice every time, and I believe that same Spirit is in us. But we need to learn how to cooperate with that Spirit. If you asked me if I ever made a wrong choice, I would readily admit that I have made plenty. I don't like making them, and I thank God for grace. But one thing is for sure—I don't practice making wrong choices. I practice making right ones, and I make fewer bad choices now than I did ten or fifteen years ago.

Be Persuaded

To make right choices, we must be persuaded of everything Jesus has told us. Paul said, "I . . . am persuaded that He is able to keep what I have committed to Him until that Day" (2 Tim. 1:12). Paul's persuasion of who Jesus was allowed him to accomplish great things. I have found that everybody is persuaded about something. We all believe one thing or another, but unless we are persuaded of the right things, and especially of the right Person, we can never go forward in our renewal process. We must be persuaded of Jesus and have a personal endearment to Him, or we will not make right choices or grow in joy, wisdom or favor.

Many men and women of God begin this process of going from a carnal to a spiritual mind. They realize they have been listening to echoes and living in the basement, and they make the first choice, as Barnabas did, to start living beyond those things. But their carnal mind is so persuaded of the wrong things that it is hard for them to believe God. Instead they believe their old emotions, old problems, old thought patterns, old experiences. They always challenge God when His Word comes to them. Their persuasions are all out of whack, and it slows them down in making right choices.

If we are not persuaded of God, how can we even begin to make right choices? The devil works overtime from the moment we are born to make sure we are not persuaded of God. I say we must believe some fundamental things about God and His trustworthiness and goodness, and then we must be willing to change our persuasions. I do not refuse to be persuaded by the things of God. Every time I learn something new from the Word I'm like a magnet. I ask the Lord if I need to change or to adapt some way. I make a choice to respond to His Word.

The Benefits

What are the benefits of making good choices? One time I spoke to a graduating high school class, and I tried to get them to understand why good choices are good. I told them this:

- Good choices open up success routes in life.

- Good choices give you confidence, like Nehemiah, to build up the wall despite opposition.

- Good choices allow your creativity and ability to flow like David's as he wrote the psalms.

- Good choices close the mouths of lions, like Daniel's good choice did.

- Good choices speed you toward the vision that is in your heart.

- Good choices make you think about *possibilities*, not about the *past*.

- Good choices can remove disappointment and anger.

- Good choices increase your potential.

- Good choices attract successful people. Moses attracted seventy elders. Jesus attracted disciples.

How do you know you've made the right choice? Deuteronomy 30:16 says you will:

- Love the Lord.
- Walk in His ways.
- Keep His Word.

In the next chapter we will look specifically at several kinds of choices we should make as we continue the process of becoming a godly person.

Chapter 8

The Power of Choice

THERE ARE A few important, basic choices we must make if we are to begin living beyond yesterday. These choices, if right, can bring us into the land of blessing— but if wrong, they will keep us away from blessing. We see examples of both right and wrong choices in the story of the prodigal son. He chose to take his inheritance from his father, leave his own home country and go into another country. He justified every bit of it. Have you ever noticed that every excuse is a good excuse when it's your excuse? He made all of his excuses and lied to himself the whole way as to why he should leave the place of blessing and go to another place. He wound up on the trash heap of humanity. But then he came to himself, and instead of being full of false pride, instead of trying to justify and prop up a failure, he humbly chose to go back to the land of blessing.

Regardless of where you are or how many mistakes you've made or the emptiness of your present situation, you can make a choice to return to blessings. God wants to lead you to a land of blessing.

Choose to Enter
the Land of Blessing

In the Book of Ruth we find the story of Naomi and her two daughters-in-law.

> Then she arose with her daughters-in-law that she might return from the country of Moab, for she had heard in the country of Moab that the LORD had visited His people by giving them bread.
>
> —RUTH 1:6

In reading the story of Naomi, you will discover that she, along with her husband Elimelech and two sons, left the place of blessing (Judah) to dwell in a place of cursing (Moab). While there, a great tragedy came into Naomi's life, and she lost her husband and two sons. She and her daughters-in-law, Ruth and Orpah, were left alone. It was at that point in her life that she made a choice to go back to the land of blessing. When Naomi chose to return to the land of blessing, Ruth, her Moabitess daughter-in-law, chose to leave her own land of cursing and relocate in the land of blessing.

Today, the place of blessing is the move of God that I have written about earlier in this book. The place of blessing is not found in the government, the stock market, mindless television entertainment or the daily newspapers. The place of blessing is not found in false religions or dead churches. The place of blessing is wherever God is moving—in your church, your life, your friend's church, your friend's life, the ministry you see on Christian television or the reports you read about revival. Make a choice to be part of this generation's revival.

Choose Against Greed

In the story of the leper Naaman, found in 2 Kings 5, we find Gehazi, the servant of Elisha, on the threshold of making a very bad choice. He was about to make the choice of greed.

> But Gehazi, the servant of Elisha the man of God, said, "Look, my master has spared Naaman this Syrian, while not receiving from his hands what he brought; but as the LORD lives. I will run after him and take something from him."
>
> —2 KINGS 5:20

This incident occurred just after Elisha had healed Naaman, who was the captain of the Syrian army and a wealthy man. In gratitude for his healing, Naaman had tried to give Elisha a lot of money, but Elisha had turned him down.

> And he [Naaman] returned to the man of God . . . and said, "Indeed, now I know that there is no God in all the earth, except in Israel; now therefore, please take a gift from your servant." But he said, "As the LORD lives, before whom I stand, I will receive nothing."
>
> —2 KINGS 5:15–16

Elisha had no problem with money, but he knew when and when not to receive an offering. But Gehazi's desire to pursue Naaman and take a gift of money in payment for his supernatural experience of healing through Elisha's ministry illustrates a second choice we must make. He made the wrong choice—because he made the choice of greed. As we can see from this example, greed rarely stands alone without its friends, deception and manipulation. Gehazi pursued Naaman out of greed, deceived him with a lie and manipulated Naaman into giving him a sum of money.

> So Gehazi pursued Naaman. When Naaman saw him running after him, he got down from the chariot to meet him, and said, "Is all well?" And he said, "All is well. My master has sent me, saying, 'Indeed, just now two young men of the sons of the prophets have come to me from the mountains of Ephraim. Please give them a talent of silver and two changes of garments.'" So Naaman said, "Please, take two talents."
>
> —2 KINGS 5:21–23

Naaman, who had a new lease on life because of his healing, was filled with the spirit of generosity, so Gehazi could have asked him for anything and received it.

If you look at Gehazi's life, you'll see that five different times God tried to promote him and train him in the supernatural. Each time, Gehazi failed the test. Why? Because the attitude of his heart was wrong. I believe that he was resentful of Elisha. I believe that Gehazi had a hard time seeing Elisha as God's chosen man, and instead saw him as Elijah's servant. Elisha had served his way into that office, and he still had the character and the heart of a servant. Gehazi looked upon that as a weakness, not realizing that the power of God works through the heart of a servant.

Have you ever noticed that Jesus did not come to the earth as a king? He did not demand his way back into heaven. He came as a humble servant and served His way back to the throne. Everybody else was offended because He was a servant, but that was the only attitude of the heart that would get Him to where He was going.

All Gehazi wanted was his next promotion, and when

it didn't come, he thought there was a weakness in Elisha. He didn't know that humble Elisha was so powerful in the Holy Spirit that when he lay down in his bed at night, God would talk to him. He didn't know that when Elisha was walking down the road singing, "This is the day that the Lord has made," the Holy Spirit was riding on his heart, saying things in his mind and in his spirit that you couldn't hear with your ear. It's a dangerous thing to envy the position of your boss. The Bible says that God is the one who puts authority in the earth. Envy blinds us to the true nature of those in authority above us.

Elisha said to him, "Gehazi, where have you been?"

And he said, "I haven't been anywhere."

Elisha said, "Well, you lied. My heart went with you. You went over there and took something from Naaman." Because he lied to the Holy Spirit and usurped Elisha's office, leprosy struck the man and stayed with his household for generations. Gehazi chose greed, and he paid the consequences.

Choose Peace

Ruth made a choice to enter into the land of blessings. Gehazi was already walking in the path of blessings, but he made a choice of greed, removing himself from blessing. In Jeremiah 29:11 we find another kind of choice. The Lord says, "For I know the thoughts that I think toward you, saith the LORD, thoughts of peace, and not of evil, to give you an expected end" (KJV). The footnote for this verse in the Online Study Bible (www.biblestudytools.net) gives this translation: " . . . to give you an end and expectation." Did you know that you ought to be expecting something good at the end of everything you do? At the end of my life, I'm expecting streets of gold. I'm going to be surfing on the glassy sea.

I once heard someone say that he had visited heaven in a vision and saw the glassy sea that the Bible talks about Revelation 4:6. To his amazement, the sea was like a giant glass dance floor where all of the saints of heaven danced before the Lord. If that's true, then I'm going to join right in.

There is one thing that God's people can expect. God has thoughts of peace toward you. He wants to give you an end and an expectation, something to hope for.

> *God has thoughts of peace toward you. He wants to give you an end and an expectation, something to hope for.*

We ought to make choices of peace. One day when I was studying, the Spirit of the Lord said to me, "God does not always require that you take the hard route." A lot of people think the easy route can't possibly be God's route because it always seems that God does things the hard way. When you have two choices in front of you, how often do you immediately eliminate the one that looks easy just because you think God couldn't possibly want it? This is the same as deciding that God always does things the hard way. But God doesn't always do things the hard way. His yoke is easy, and His burden is light. He's not into blowing you away with the most difficult circumstance every day. Thank God, I've been through the valley, but as I said before, I'm not buying real estate there.

God's thoughts toward you are thoughts of peace. There may be times when God tells you to do something the hard way—in the natural. But if He tells you to do something in the natural, He will go before you to prepare the way. The hard way is not necessarily God's way. That thought will set you free.

Choose to Accept Counsel

Another type of choice is found in 1 Kings 12. Solomon had died and his son, Rehoboam, had come to the throne. A lot of people wanted to know how he would rule. Would he be like David, who ruled justly? Or would he be like Solomon, who became a very difficult ruler?

> Then King Rehoboam consulted the elders who stood before his father Solomon while he still lived, and he said, "How do you advise me to answer these people?" And they spoke to him, saying, "If you will be a servant to these people today, and serve them, and answer them, and speak good words to them, then they will be your servants forever."
>
> — I KINGS 12:6–7

That's good advice, in my opinion. I think every pastor on the planet ought to hear those words. I feel so blessed as a pastor to have men who have counseled me out of their years of experience. That's exactly what Rehoboam had the opportunity to do right here, but the Scripture says that he rejected that counsel:

> But he rejected the advice which the elders had given him, and consulted the young men who had grown up with him, who stood before him. And he said to them, "What advice do you give? How should we answer this people who have spoken to me, saying, 'Lighten the yoke which your father put on us'?"
> Then the young men who had grown up with him spoke to him, saying, "Thus you should speak

> to this people who have spoken to you, saying,
> 'Your father made our yoke heavy, but you make it
> lighter on us'—thus you shall say to them, 'My little
> finger shall be thicker than my father's waist! And
> now, whereas my father put a heavy yoke on you, I
> will add to your yoke; my father chastised you with
> whips, but I will chastise you will scourges!'"
>
> —1 KINGS 12:8–11

Rehoboam made a downright bad choice. I call this the choice to accept counsel that is contrary to the fruit of the Spirit. We ought not make choices given to us by friends who are not anointed. We have to have wise counsel from people who are anointed. The Bible says that there is safety in a multitude of counselors (Prov. 24:6). There is a difference between counsel and advice. Anyone can give advice from their head, but how many can give wise counsel from their heart? Learning the difference ought to be at the forefront of our efforts.

Choose to Give Godly Counsel

Just as we receive godly counsel, we should be prepared to give it.

> Peter and John went up together to the temple at
> the hour of prayer, the ninth hour. And a certain
> man lame from his mother's womb was carried,
> whom they laid daily at the gate of the temple
> which is called Beautiful, to ask alms from those
> who entered the temple; who, seeing Peter and
> John about to go into the temple, asked for alms.
> And fixing his eyes on him, with John, Peter said,
> "Look at us." So he gave them his attention,
> expecting to receive something from them. Then
> Peter said, "Silver and gold I do not have, but what

I do have I give you: In the name of Jesus Christ of Nazareth, rise up and walk." And he took him by the right hand and lifted him up, and immediately his feet and ankle bones received strength.

—ACTS 3:1–7

Did you know that God will open the door for you to give godly counsel? But at the same time, the devil will try to intimidate you and tell you not to say anything. He'll try to convince you that people will label you a fanatic or an interloper. Watch for those times when God opens the door, and then go ahead and give godly advice. Don't be afraid of the crowd. You might be in a room where everybody else is giving advice contrary to your godly advice. The Scripture says that there is an anointing on the Christian to choose the good and refuse the evil. So go ahead and choose the godly advice. God is looking for people who will rise up in their generation and give godly advice.

God is looking for people who will rise up in their generation and give godly advice.

Don't Make Choices Based on Peer Pressure

Another choice we have to make is to go against the crowd when directing our own lives. We need to apply that godly counsel to ourselves and not be ruled by what other people—even our friends—say. In 1 Samuel 15, Samuel had rebuked Saul for disobeying God. Saul replied, "I have sinned, for I have transgressed the commandment of the LORD and your words, because I feared the people and obeyed their voice" (v. 24). Saul made a choice based on peer pressure.

Almost without exception, choices you make because of peer pressure will be the wrong ones. Don't make choices based on "everyone's doing it." In reality, everyone is not doing it.

Elijah had that problem. He thought that everybody was serving Baal, and he made a horrible choice—he fled from the land of blessing:

> And there he went into a cave, and spent the night in that place; and behold, the word of the LORD came to him, and He said to him, "What are you doing here, Elijah?" So he said, "I have been very zealous for the LORD God of hosts; for the children of Israel have forsaken Your covenant, torn down Your altars, and killed Your prophets with the sword. I alone am left; and they seek to take my life."
>
> —1 KINGS 19:9–10

God had to set him straight and say, "Yet I have reserved seven thousand in Israel, all whose knees have not bowed to Baal, and every mouth that has not kissed him" (v. 18). If you keep reading, you will discover that all of the people of Judah had not bowed to Baal either.

Choose to Make Covenants

> "And if it seems evil to you to serve the LORD, choose for yourselves this day whom you will serve, whether the gods which your fathers served that were on the other side of the River, or the gods of the Amorites, in whose land you dwell. But as for me and my house, we will serve the LORD." . . . And

the people said to Joshua, "The LORD our God we
will serve, and His voice we will obey!" So Joshua
made a covenant with the people that day.
—JOSHUA 24:15, 24–25

We need to make choices to make covenants. I believe
there are three kinds of covenants that you can make.
The first one is a *church covenant*—a relationship that's
based upon spiritual principles, or spiritual truth, with
Jesus as the center of it. When you make a church
covenant, or when God adds you to a church, you need
to be supportive. You need to be faithful to come to
church. I learned a long time ago that I cannot pastor
anybody effectively to whom I cannot preach. We need
to be faithful to come to the house of God, because it is
the Word of God that causes us to grow. Making that
covenant can only help you.

When you make a church covenant, you need to be
faithful to those men and women who are around you.
This is a *body covenant*—one in which you are faithful
by praying for those in your church family. That doesn't
mean to go lay hands on every person. But you are to lift
up in prayer the men and women of the family to which
God has called you to be a part. Make good choices in
what you say about your church and the people in your
church, especially about your pastor. There's a spiritual
impact on your life if you talk negatively about the
people with whom you worship, because you are in
covenant with them.

I can tell what parents talk about based upon their
children. Children who love their pastor almost without
exception have parents who also love the pastor. If you
want your children to grow up full of faith and full of
the Holy Spirit, then don't get in the car and talk about
how the music was too loud or how rude the nursery
worker at church was. Junior is in the back seat listening

to everything you say, and you are programming his little mind and heart. When he gets old enough to make his own decisions he'll say he doesn't want to come to church. Demonstrate the values of a church covenant and a body covenant to your children.

The third type of covenant we make is a *relationship covenant*. When my wife and I entered into marriage, we made a covenant together that whatever might come, we were going to continue our marriage until Jesus comes. Whatever you do with your life, make sure you enter into covenant relationships, first with your family and then with certain godly people around you. They will make you stronger, help you to mature and keep you in the land of blessing. If you pray about this, God will guide you to the right people and give you healthy relationships that will be of far greater value than your career or your accomplishments.

Having looked at several basic choices we need to make to live beyond yesterday, let's now look at the process we go through in renewing our minds so that our iniquities and echoes can be overcome for good.

Chapter 9

Renewing the Mind

IN JOHN 3:6, Jesus says, "That which is born of the flesh is flesh, and that which is born of the Spirit is spirit." This is Christianity 101. It tells us that all who are born again have been born twice: once in the flesh, once in the Spirit. When you were born in the flesh all those years ago, your natural reflexes immediately showed themselves. As soon as you came out of the womb, you wanted to eat. Those of you who are mothers know what I mean. Infants have a sucking reflex. They are born of the flesh, and they immediately begin to relate to flesh.

The older you get, you notice that you never lose that reflex of eating. Of all the reflexes that seem to have been ingrained in you, eating is the most basic.

According to the Bible, every person has two minds— a carnal mind and a spiritual mind.

> That the righteous requirement of the law might be fulfilled in us who do not walk according to the flesh but according to the Spirit. For those who live

> according to the flesh set their minds on the things
> of the flesh, but those who live according to the
> Spirit, the things of the Spirit. For to be carnally
> minded is death, but to be spiritually minded is life
> and peace.
>
> —ROMANS 8:4–6

According to Romans 8, you can be a Christian and still be carnally minded. If you want to fall back into carnality, you can choose that at any moment. God cannot keep you from making that choice. Before we chose to allow Jesus to come into our lives, we were carnal men with carnal bodies. As such, we were in the dying process. But now the Scripture says that we are in the living process.

Programmed by God

To be carnally minded is to have a death mind. Your soul or mind in its carnal state, according to Romans 8:5-6, was programmed by your flesh up to the moment that you were born again. Your flesh was at enmity with God, not subject to the law of God, and could not be. So the Holy Spirit was not programming you before you were born again. You were programming yourself and learning by the things of this fallen realm.

When God created Adam, He gave him the ability to communicate with his environment by way of smell, sight, taste, hearing and touch. Those senses allowed him to program his mind, his soul. God breathed His Spirit into the man, allowing Him to talk to Adam on a spiritual level. Thus Adam was programmed by the Spirit of God.

Then sin came, and the Bible states emphatically that Adam died. God had spoken to Adam about the tree of the knowledge of good and evil, saying, "But of the tree of the knowledge of good and evil you shall not eat, for in the day that you eat of it you shall surely die" (Gen. 2:17). The Hebrew literally says, "In the day that you eat, or disobey God, the day that you make the wrong choice and sin comes in, it's going to sway you, and in dying you shall die."

The moment that Adam and Eve sinned, they did not physically drop dead, but spiritually they were separated from that place of unity with God, which is spiritual death. Spiritual death produces eventual physical death. By the same token, spiritual life produces physical life.

For all men since the Fall of Adam, the soulish man is programmed by the fallen nature or by the re-created nature. When you were born again, you regained what Adam lost in the Fall. Since you have received salvation, you have the curse in reverse. God has the ability to talk to you and teach you the things of God. Your spiritual mind is being programmed into the nature of God.

There is a carnal mind, and there is a spiritual mind. Most of you are aware of your two minds. For example, perhaps every time an attractive man or woman walks by, you almost break your neck to catch a glance of that person. That's your carnal mind at work. But then your spirit mind rises up inside of you and says, "Wait a minute, I'm not involved with lust. God's given me a Holy Spirit mate, someone to walk alongside me all the days of my life. My mate satisfies the needs of my life, and my world is full."

Or you may get an unexpected bill in the mail and think, *Praise God, my God supplies all my needs according to His riches in glory by Christ Jesus.* That's your spiritual mind working. But you may have another thought: *We're going to starve to death. We will never have enough money to pay the bills.* Remember that it's as easy to believe the voice of the Spirit and the mind of the Spirit as it is to believe the mind of the flesh. You can be carnally minded, or you can be spiritually minded. It is a choice. God clearly laid out that choice when He said:

> I have set before you life and death, blessing and cursing; therefore choose life.
>
> —DEUTERONOMY 30:19

We recently had a family over to our house for supper. Their precious little daughter was sitting in the high chair eating carrots and being cute, when all of a sudden an odor permeated the room. We knew it wasn't any of the food that had been prepared. That precious little baby needed to be changed.

Imagine for a moment that this mother lifted her baby from the high chair, took her into the changing room, grabbed a clean diaper, *put it over the old diaper* and then came back reporting that the baby was all cleaned up. Within seconds, the rest of us would have known that although she appeared to have had a change— something crucial had not changed.

God doesn't want to put a covering over our sin any more. He wants to take away the old mind and its iniquities entirely. Aren't you glad He doesn't just slap a new diaper over the old one? Aren't you glad we don't have to walk around all day with the scent of sin hanging over us? Aren't you glad that God will change or renew us every time we make the choice to be changed? Like a baby who needs to be changed again and again, we will need to cast off the old mind many times. But the rewards are worth it.

Why Serve God?

A lot of people serve God legalistically. They have learned how to go through the motions of serving Him, but before long, they settle on their own ways. They forget that everything they own and everything they are belong to Him. They start telling God how His hair is supposed to be worn, how He's supposed to dress, what music He should listen to. They create rules for living that justify their actions and make them feel as if everything is all right. In essence, they are wearing clean diapers on the outside, but they still carry the stench of sin on the inside.

I grew up in church, and I am thankful for my spiritual heritage. But as a boy I rarely heard messages on grace. Preachers were afraid that if they preached about grace somebody would say, "He believes in that once-saved-always-saved stuff. He believes in greasy grace."

The only way to serve effectively is by renewing your mind in His Word and by His Spirit so that you serve Him by nature—your renewed spiritual nature.

Some of the most bitter people I've known were people who were already born again. If you don't understand the principle of the renewing of the mind, you will become hard and legalistic in a short period of time. You will create a lifestyle that attempts to compensate for the failings of the internal man that has not been renewed. You will stack your hair a certain way, wear your clothes a certain way and proclaim, "We are going to church, come rain or shine." But if your heart isn't changed and your mind hasn't been renewed, you will become as bitter as gall. Although you do everything you know to do in the flesh to be a born-again, Spirit-filled

Christian, something will still be wrong inside of you.

Other people serve God emotionally. When they go through a hard time, they start crying out to God. Only when the bills stack up, the utilities turn off, their marriage washes up on the beach or their kids go crazy, do they seek God with their whole heart. God will hear you when you cry out like that. But why live from crisis to crisis when you can overcome those things before they become so critical? It's better to live for God with an even, steady keel in the Lord than it is to drift from squall to squall.

The only way to serve effectively is by renewing your mind in His Word and by His Spirit so that you serve Him by nature—your renewed spiritual nature. Romans 8 says:

> There is therefore now no condemnation to those who are in Christ Jesus, who do not walk according to the flesh, but according to the Spirit. For the law of the Spirit of life in Christ Jesus has made me free from the law of sin and death. For what the law could not do in that it was weak through the flesh, God did.
>
> —Romans 8:1–3

Notice how the Law dealt with the flesh. If you try to serve God through your flesh, or because you feel like you have to, or because you are trying to keep from going to hell, you are serving God under the Law. There is a much better way to serve God, and that is to embark on the adventure of renewing your mind.

Fighting to Win

I don't know about you, but I like to win. I'm not too competitive in the flesh anymore, but I am extremely competitive in the spirit. The older you get, the more you find out you're not as quick as you used to be in the flesh. I remember as a boy growing up in school that I was extremely competitive in the flesh. I couldn't stand to lose at anything. If I lost, I'd say, "I'll get you next time, I guarantee you." But after a while, competition in the flesh gave way to faith.

But in the spirit it's different. The more that I press into the kingdom of God and the more that God renews my mind, the more I refuse to accept defeat in the spirit. The further I go along in the Word of God, the more I understand about the truths of the kingdom and the more I expect people to be healed when I lay hands on them in Jesus' name.

I am the same way when it comes to renewing my mind. I want to win, and I will take nothing less. Any man or any woman, to enable change, must desire it desperately. It's like a salmon swimming upstream. All of your life you've gone with the flow of carnality. Now you are swimming against the current, and you must keep a sincere desire to keep going.

After we have made the decision to make good choices rather than bad ones, we begin to apply that decision to our lives. We have talked about the echo chamber. We have talked about living our lives in the living room rather than in the basement or on the rooftop. We have talked about speaking with the voice of faith. We have discussed iniquity and how to overcome it. We've seen how breaking free of the old man is a process and that we are required to make right choices if we are to succeed. In the last chapter we took a broad look at healthy choices.

Now the rubber hits the road. Will you live beyond yesterday, or will these words just tickle your ears? Will you renew your mind according to the biblical prescription, or will the old mind continue to control you?

After the Flesh

The mind is the battleground of renewal, and thoughts are the weapons of war. Thoughts have a way of growing and maturing into full-blown realities, if we let them. Thoughts become opinions, which become words, which become actions, which become sin—and the wages of that sin is death. Once a thought has jumped out of your mind and into the flesh, you create a whole new set of problems. The healthy thing to do is deal with it in the mind. You have to challenge that sinful thought on its own battlefield.

> *The mind is the battleground of renewal, and thoughts are the weapons of war.*

Your greatest asset (and possibly your greatest liability, depending on how you use it)—your mind—is positioned between your ears. The mind is our weapon against the echoes of the past. A thought doesn't have the right to be in your head just because it's a thought. Paul said, ". . . casting down arguments and every high thing that exalts itself against the knowledge of God, bringing every thought into captivity to the obedience of Christ" (2 Cor. 10:5). You must be ready to tell intruding thoughts, "You can't stay in my life." Take dominion over them. Start challenging your thoughts instead of letting your thoughts challenge you.

I made a decision years ago to analyze my thoughts and to refuse to let them control me. I decided to let my spirit man control my thought life. It's a personal discipline, something the Bible calls *the spirit of self-control.*

Ephesians 5 talks about being washed with the water of the Word. Personally, I try to get brainwashed every day!

But I'm careful to use the pure water of the Word. Everybody is getting brainwashed. The question is whether it's pure or muddy water that's washing over their minds.

Thoughts are like visitors, whether they be welcome or unwelcome. You have no real control over who comes to your house and knocks on the door. But you have control over who comes in. It's the same way in the spirit. You may not have control over what you think, but you have control over what you re-think. You don't have any control over how your life was in the past, because it's done and gone. But you have all the control in the world over whether or not your past life is controlling your present life today.

We need to learn to discern which thoughts are of God, and which are not. Isaiah 55:8 says, "'My thoughts are not your thoughts, nor are your ways My ways,' says the LORD. 'For as the heavens are higher than the earth, so are My ways higher than your ways, and My thoughts than your thoughts.'" Philippians 2:5 says, "Let this mind be in you which was also in Christ Jesus."

In another scripture we read, "For the weapons of our warfare are not carnal but mighty in God for pulling down strongholds" (2 Cor. 10:4). Strongholds are established in people's minds. Strongholds are strategic systems of thought—patterns of lifestyle that get formed in people's minds. Strongholds lead to defeat, lifelessness, lack of joy, lack of unity and lack of peace. But the Bible says that the weapons of our warfare are not carnal, but mighty through God to the pulling down of these systematic thought patterns, ideas and concepts, inherited many times by association of families and friends.

God's Perfect Will

God has a perfect will for your life, but if you do not become transformed by the renewing of your mind, you will never enter into it. The Bible says that there is a good, acceptable and perfect will of God. I personally believe God's will for my life is one all-encompassing plan. I do not believe that there are several choices of God's will for a person's life, like having door number one, door number two and door number three. Yes, a person can be out of the perfect will of God, and the mercy and the grace of God will still work for them to some degree. But I believe the will of God is good, acceptable and perfect. No one can claim to have been in the perfect will of God for his or her life *at all moments.* I can't, and you can't either. How grateful I am for the grace of God that sustains us when we are in a position of seeking to know God's will or are pressing God to "rearrange" His will to suit our own plans or desires.

> God will never steal from you; He will only add to you. He will bless you, never curse you.

The Bible says that actual change—transformation—takes place as our minds are renewed, moving us closer and closer to that perfect will of God. That's where we are headed right now. God's will is good and very acceptable. God will never steal from you; He will only add to you. He will bless you, never curse you.

The Seven Rs of Renewal

Responsibility

If you are going to renew your mind, you have to make a decision to take responsibility for your thought life. You can't accept every thought that comes into your head. If you ponder every thought that tries to occupy your mind, your adversary the devil, the god of this world, will be able to entertain you with evil continually. Your five senses record the ingredients of your thoughts. It only takes the smell, sound, taste, feel or sight of evil to program evil into your thought life. You have to make a decision to take responsibility for your thoughts.

You can't meditate on the things that are not good or not of God and still renew your mind. You must "[bring] every thought into captivity to the obedience of Christ" (2 Cor. 10:5). As you think in your heart, that's the way it's going to be.

I do not like people to get up in church and talk about their past life or the way it was before they were saved. While testimony times have some value, in many cases people talk for forty-five minutes about their experiences with drugs, prison, adultery, illegal and immoral activities— all the things the world does. Then at the last minute they take a few moments and say that they met Jesus, were born again and are now having a lot of fun. They spend vastly more time discussing what their flesh used to do. By the time they finish, you have an audience of people whose minds are filled with sinful images and stories.

You don't need to put such thoughts into your mind— or anybody else's. Many of those testimonies are carnal desires that have not been put down in the people who are talking. That's why it's so dangerous to put a new convert in front of people as though that person were some kind of star. A new convert has a long way to go to get a renewed mind. Treating new converts as though they were perfect the moment they are born again hinders the process of the renewing of their minds.

Ephesians 4:22 exhorts us to "put off, concerning your former conduct, the old man which grows corrupt." The phrase "put off" carries the connotation of taking your coat and slinging it off. We have to put effort into having the mind of Christ and resisting the carnal mind. If you are waiting to experience a Holy Spirit moment that totally eradicates your carnal mind—with its old thoughts, old deceitfulness, old ideas, old attitudes, old actions—you can forget it. God said that you have to put it off yourself. To do that you have to have new thought patterns. The way that you get new thought patterns is to meditate on the Word of God, meditate on the ways of God, feed yourself the Word of God, pray in the understanding, pray in the Spirit and fellowship with people who are endeavoring to do these same things.

Christians like myself enjoy spiritual experiences. We profess, "We don't live by feelings; we live by faith." But in reality, many Christians who are filled with the Holy Spirit live by feelings. Thank God for feelings. I love it when the Holy Spirit seems to fill the place up and everybody is experiencing God's holy presence and getting filled with joy. Personally, I am a spiritual-experience addict. I have to have the moving of the Holy Spirit to make me feel complete. But I also resist living by my feelings. When the Holy Spirit moves, I enjoy it; but when He doesn't, I keep right on going in God. When you live by feelings, you get the good and the bad. Old feelings try to come up, and God says that you have to put them down.

If you want more spiritual experiences, make a decision to put off the things of the flesh. Allow more room in your life for God to visit you. You will never maximize the potential of God's visitation in your life until you put off the things of the flesh.

Re-think

We have to be willing to re-think thought patterns. Some people say, "I'm kind of old now, and you know, you can't teach an old dog new tricks." You're not a dog.

You have a mind, will, emotions and intellect. You are constantly adding to your knowledge. If what you've lived by for the last twenty-five years did not get you victory, you had better be willing to re-think your "tricks" and establish them according to the Word of God. Start trying to find out where you have been "missing it" in your own personal philosophy and ideas. Be willing to re-think yesterday and the ideas or opinions that have brought you to this point of your life.

For example, get rid of those secret cavern areas of your mind that you don't want anybody else to know about. The Bible plainly says that the secret things will come to light. They will ultimately manifest in your life. I believe this fact accounts for what our society calls "the middle-age crazies" or a "midlife crisis." I've

> *You will never maximize the potential of God's visitation in your life until you put off the things of the flesh.*

heard people say, "I think they are going through a middle-age crazy." I don't call it that—I call it a mind full of sin. It happens when a person has meditated for forty-five or fifty years on sin, and suddenly, it slays them.

You can't justify sin by calling it a biological change in your body. You have to make a decision to re-think your old ways lest they come back and kill you. Thank God that you don't have to cheat on your spouse or destroy your family. The Word of God is stronger than that. All you have to do is to renew your mind, even if you're fifty years old.

Hebrews 10:38–39 says, "Now the just shall live by faith; but if anyone draws back, My soul has no pleasure in him. But we are not of those who draw back to perdition, but of those who believe to the saving of the soul." You may not lose your salvation by slipping back into old habits, but you can sure draw back from it. The Bible says that we are not to be those who draw back—we are to move ever forward "to the saving of the soul."

In my early experiences growing up in the church, it seemed impossible to stay saved from daylight to dark. If you committed one sin, that was it. Thank God, that's not the way it really is. When you were born again, you were sealed by the spirit of promise until the day of redemption. But unless you are willing to re-think your old thought patterns and throw out the dangerous ones, you could slip back into perdition and be lost. I don't say that to frighten you, but to encourage you to take your thoughts seriously before they take you captive.

Reject the old

The third R of renewal is learning to reject the old, including old thought patterns, old ideas, old ways, old phrases and old doctrines. If they are contrary to the Word of God, reject them immediately. Whenever thoughts about the things of the old man present themselves in your mind, say, "No, in the name of Jesus, I reject that. That's not a part of my life." Speak the Word of God to yourself in response to that sinful thought. If you don't know the Word of God, follow the advice of Ephesians 4 and sit under the tutelage of an apostle, prophet, evangelist, pastor or teacher who is able to help you become mature. One of the most important things for every believer—the reason God put you in a local church—is to allow your mind to be renewed. Make a decision to reject the ideas, thoughts and fantasies of yesterday.

Many husbands and wives suffer desperately in their own personal relationships because they have never rejected the things of yesterday in which they were once involved. They do not take responsibility for their thoughts, and they do not renew their minds. It's an act of the will. Choose this day whom you will serve.

Ephesians 4:25–5:7 gives a great synopsis of the old ways that must be put off. Let's review these things:

- *Stop lying.* This also means to stop telling yourself that you are what God has delivered you from.

- *Don't sin in your anger.* Make a decisive choice against that iniquity in your life.

- *Don't give place to the devil* to fill you with condemnation or conviction. Clean it up immediately, and once it's clean, don't allow him to convince you that you are still under that condemnation.

- *Never identify yourself with a known sin,* and stop identifying with past sins. If you were an alcoholic, abuser, cheat or spouse abuser, don't identify with that sin anymore. The lie is that the sin still defines you. The truth is that you are the righteousness of God in Christ Jesus.

- *Put away obvious sin.* Take stealing, for example, which encompasses much more than the theft of a physical object. Don't steal a person's virginity, loyalty or money. Make a decision never to violate what belongs to someone else.

- *Let your work glorify God.* If you work on computers, don't create pornographic sites. If you are a nuclear physicist, don't make bombs. Make power plants instead. Don't use your skill for something evil.

In this passage of Scripture, Paul also explains the importance of marriage partners helping one another in the renewing process. It will require that you re-think your relationship, conversations, attitudes and actions toward each other. If you are having trouble communicating with each other, you need to establish a pattern of godly communication.

At first in this renewing process, communication may be difficult. Consider the circumstances that have come up because of individual inferiorities and weaknesses. Each partner will have to re-think old blame games and put-downs, arguments and annoyances. Begin to affirm aloud: "I love to talk to my wife. She is such a good listener. I love to listen to my husband talk. He is such a good talker. I love my children and my home." Set some new habits. Turn off the television; play family games; sit around and talk. Do anything that opens up new lines of healthy communication and causes old ways to fade away. Prepare yourself in advance for attacks from the enemy, and have new habits in place. Be willing to re-think the old and to critique yourself by the Word of God.

Verse 7 of Ephesians 5 says, "Therefore do not be partakers with them"—the fornicator, unclean person, covetous man, idolater and deceiver. The people with whom we hang around are critically important to how successful we will be at renewing our minds. We all know what it is like to hang around people who parrot the same self-serving clichés to each other—clichés that lack the power to deliver you out of them. Choose to be with people who are in the process of being set free.

If you are going to renew your mind, you may have to disassociate yourself from people who are not trying to change into the image of the Lord. People who are not in the process of change will despise the fact that you are pressing toward the mark. By their carnal nature, they will be at enmity with change and, consciously or unconsciously, will try to keep you from changing. If they can keep you from changing, it will justify their own regressive state. Separate from and disassociate with people who are not willing to make the journey with you.

You may say, "But they are nice people." It has nothing to do with being nice or good or bad. Our righteousness, or niceness, is as filthy rags in God's sight. If a nice person could go to heaven just for being a nice person, Jesus would not have come and died for us. God is not just trying to make you nice. He's trying to change you.

Perhaps as important as your social group is the kind of music to which you listen. Music is always the voice of a kingdom, and every kingdom has its own music. If you go to Ireland, they play the Irish hymn. If you come to the United States, they play the national anthem.

In other words, don't think about where you came from; think about where you're going.

If you go to Germany, they play the German anthem. Music is the voice or language of a culture. It is kingdom communication. Whenever you hear music, you should ask yourself, "What kingdom is that communicating coming from and going to?" Is it giving praise to God? Or is it pledging allegiance to a different set of values? What do the words say? What thoughts do the rhythm and melody conjure up in you?

Music will either help you or hinder you in renewing your mind. It goes right into your heart and can change the way you think. You don't need to take the money that God has blessed you with and throw it away on music that will pollute your thoughts. We are kings and priests unto our God, and the music we hear should be fit for a king. Don't let the local disc jockey determine your thoughts.

In Philippians Paul admonishes, "Whatever things are pure, whatever things are lovely, whatever things are of good report, if there is any virtue and if there is anything praiseworthy—meditate on these things" (Phil. 4:8). In other words, don't think about where you came from; think about where you're going. When you want God, you can't live like where you came from.

Too many Christians have been delivered *to* something, and they still think as they did where they came *from*. They talk as they did where they came from. They hang around yesterday's friends. They listen to yesterday's music. They dwell on yesterday's thoughts and goals. Whom are they fooling? They must systematically reject everything that is negative from their past.

God wants to synergize His nature and character with ours. He literally wants to live in us. Our bodies—our ears, our mouths, our eyes—are the temples of the Holy Spirit. Jesus has intertwined Himself in my spirit, and I have intertwined myself with Him. Yes, I still have an old nature, but I have yielded to the new nature that is now come upon me. I have died to my old man, and my new identity is Christ in me, the hope of glory.

The greatest day in your life is when you can look in the mirror and see more than you. You need to see the heart of God and the Spirit of God that are now living inside of you. The nature of God begins to overtake even your most obstinate physical features and make you glow with His radiance.

Review the new

It is important to review the new. Meditate and speak the Word. Constantly think on it in response to every area of weakness in your life. Review what God says about your life. You cannot have a war going on inside of you and expect to receive from God, so you must review the new and reject the old. The Book of James says that a double-minded man is unstable in all his ways. Let not that man think he will receive anything from God. (See James 1:7–8.)

Reviewing the new might seem tedious, but it is really the greatest opportunity you have to change because it is woven into every minute of our lives. When the Word of God is coursing through your mind like a river, you see every situation differently. It gives life a different flavor. Suddenly you can contribute positively to the people around you, because God will give you wisdom, grace and love. By reviewing the new, you are putting new treasure in your heart. It's a life-long process.

Scripture says, "A good man out of the good treasure of his heart brings forth good; and an evil man out of the evil treasure of his heart brings forth evil" (Luke 6:45). Before you were saved, you had evil things programmed into you. When you were saved, you began the lifelong process of exchanging the treasure of your heart for godly treasure. Many people get saved, filled with the Holy Spirit, delivered from drugs, alcohol, cigarettes or pornography and live in the strength of the emotional part of that spiritual experience for a period of time, perhaps thirty or forty days. Praise God, they were delivered! But they fail to put something new into the treasury, and before long, old thoughts come back out of their treasury to once again invade their minds. Soon they fall back into the world. Other people struggle with a cycle of sin and repentance for decades, maybe their whole lives. Why? They have not made a decision to review the new and replace their treasure.

What are you putting into the treasury of your heart? Is it good or evil? God said that you have to make the decision to bring something new and something good out of the treasure of your heart. The only way to get something good out is to put something good in. Review the new. Stop putting in evil thoughts, ideas, actions and words. Start putting in good.

Resound the Word

A fourth R to renewal is learning to resound the Word of God. Speak the Word of God into your inner man and life.

Before I became a pastor, I was a member of the Masons. (I have since come to the understanding that that organization is not of God.) But as a member of the Masons I learned something about myself: I have a good memory. I had been required by that organization to memorize large portions of text. In that process I found out that I could remember things.

I'm no different than any other man, but I was forced to apply myself and see where my limits were. I was surprised by what I could memorize. I believe everyone has a great memory, but many suffer from mental laziness. At least, that was my problem.

Now I have made a decision to commit to memory as much of the Word of God as I can. I'm comfortable memorizing whole passages. I do so because I want my mind to be renewed by the Word of God so that I can fulfill the call of God on my life.

You need that same desire in your heart. Speak, resound and meditate on the Word of God continually. Declare that your bad marriage relationship will be restored. Declare that you and your household are going to be saved. Declare that your children will grow up like olive shoots around your table. They will rise up one day and call you blessed. Like arrows are in the hands of a mighty man, so are the children of your youth or of your womb. Declare that your family abides in the secret place of the Most High, under the shadow of the Almighty. Assert that although a thousand may fall by your side and ten thousand by your right side, danger will not come near you.

When you resound the Word of God, it imprints something across your mind. One day, while visiting a print shop, I was fascinated by a machine I saw there. It looked like a large copy machine. I asked to see how it worked. The employees laid a metal plate over the image they wanted to have imprinted on it, closed the lid and hit the start button. A bright light flashed inside the machine, and when they lifted up the lid, that impression had been burned into the plate, which then became the master plate from which they print many more copies.

The light of the gospel is the same way. When you begin to speak the Word of God and resound that Word into yourself, it burns into your spirit. Regardless of what anything says, your mind—the control center of your life—will constantly be speaking the truth.

In Matthew 12:34, Jesus speaks to the Pharisees, saying, "Brood of vipers! How can you, being evil, speak good things? For out of the abundance of the heart the mouth speaks." Isn't it interesting that the tongue is tied to the heart?

The devil has tried to suppress the confession of our faith in the body of Christ. The Word exhorts us to hold fast the confession of our faith. We are exhorted to speak the Word of God. Meditate on the Word. The word *meditate* in the Hebrew means "to mutter." Speak the Word of God constantly with your mouth, because when you do, the Word of God will come through into your new, re-created spirit and will be written upon the table of your mind.

Rejoice

The sixth R is to rejoice. When you rejoice in God and rejoice in the Word over your life, you've taken responsibility. You are rejecting the old. You're renewing your mind in God. You're re-thinking things, and you're resounding the truth. Then you begin to rejoice in the God of your salvation.

You can rejoice in God the same way you rejoiced in things as a child. Some of you remember the joy of anticipating a trip to the circus or to the ice cream shop. Just thinking about it makes you smile. Make a decision to rejoice over your husband, your wife, your children, your church and your relationship in God. Rejoice because your thought life has changed. Rejoice at the progress you are making.

Results

A seventh R to renewal is results. I like to call it *becoming a fruit inspector in your life.* In this way you keep yourself on track by seeing if there has, indeed, been a change.

Here are six quick ways to know you that you are being renewed in your mind.

Commitment—One of the great character traits of men and women who are being changed into the image of Jesus Christ is that they become extremely committed to the things of God and to godly relationships. Be committed to the house of God, to the work of God that's in your life and to your relationships with other Christians. People need to know that you are committed. Cindy and I have been married twenty-four years, and we are committed to each other. You couldn't get me to say anything bad about my wife—even if there were anything bad I could say, which there isn't. Never say anything negative about the commitments in your life.

Discipline—Jesus said, "If you abide in My word, you are My disciples indeed. And you shall know the truth, and the truth shall make you free" (John 8:31–32). In another place Jesus said that those who do not pick up their cross

148

and follow Him cannot be His disciples. One way to know that change is coming inside is by your desire for discipleship. You know you're changing when, as you ride in your car, you're thinking, *There are things in my life that I've got to change, and I'm going to do it, in the name of Jesus.* You've taken control of your thoughts. You have a stubborn persistence that you are not going to be ruled by anything of your past life. You are not going to let something that someone did to you when you were a child rule you. Your life is no longer under the control of other people, but under the discipline of Christ. Only He will captivate your thoughts, goals and imaginations.

Holiness—Hebrews 12:14 says that without holiness you will not see God. You have to be holy even as He is holy. (See 1 Peter 1:15-16.) Here's a thumbnail definition of holiness: You are holy when you don't want to have anything to do with sin or anything that taints the reputation of a holy God. You will abstain from the appearance of evil because it will put a negative remark against the God who loves you and bought you. You don't want to make someone else lust after you, and you don't want to lust after someone else. You don't want to be deceived, and you don't want to deceive someone else. You don't want someone to be mad at you, and you don't want to be mad at someone else. You'll go to all kinds of extremes to love others and be loved back.

> *You are holy when you don't want to have anything to do with sin or anything that taints the reputation of a holy God.*

The Scripture says to guard your heart with all diligence, for out of it flow the forces of life (Prov. 4:23). Does your mouth exemplify holiness? Do you have what the Scripture calls "perverse lips"? You will never be a progressive person if you have a regressive mouth.

What about your eyes? Are they holy? Job said, "I have made a covenant with my eyes" (Job 31:1). I think that's the prettiest verse in the Bible. The next time an attractive man or woman walks by you, say, "I'm going to be like Job."

Generosity—Being renewed in the spirit of the mind breaks stinginess and greediness, pride and competition. A spirit of generosity comes about you. Proverbs 11:25 says that the generous soul shall be made rich. As you are renewed, you will want to bless somebody. You will want to be bountiful with everything that you have.

Loyalty—How many are loyal to the kingdom of God? Jude 3 says, "I found it necessary to write to you exhorting you to contend earnestly for the faith which was once for all delivered to the saints." Be loyal to the work of faith that was delivered unto the saints. Contend for it. Refuse to compromise. Be loyal toward the body of Christ. Be loyal toward your pastors. Be loyal toward your spouse. Be loyal toward your children.

As a pastor, I don't like a husband or a wife coming to me and running their spouse down. As a matter of fact, they'll only do it one time in my presence, because either I'll heal them or make them so uncomfortable by refusing to side with them that they will never want to talk to me again. I've had people leave my church because I said, "Don't say that about your husband or wife. God says that you hate your own flesh if you hate your spouse."

You know your mind is being renewed if you guard your family. You won't let the forces of death get in there. You won't complain about your spouse. You won't look at your house and say, "I hate this thing." You will manage your family like an expert and loving manager. I've told many people that I don't *pastor my family—I father my family.* I manage my house. I don't get up in the morning and tell my kids, "Up against the wall, I've got a word for you." I have sat down with every one of my children many times and said, "The Spirit of the Lord told me this," or "I feel this in my spirit." But I try to be a gentle and loving father. I want to nurture my family, not control them.

Recognize the will of God—People who are renewed in their minds don't get deceived as often by the devil. As you put the Word of God in you, your thoughts line up toward God as if they were magnetized. You recognize deception and can quickly reject it. You become firm in your stand.

When a man or a woman has a renewed mind, is filled with the Holy Spirit and obeys the will of God, that person becomes a tremendously attractive force to the world. Jesus said it like this: "And I, if I am lifted up from the earth, will draw all peoples to Myself" (John 12:32). The most awesome person on the face of the earth is a man or a woman whose body, soul and spirit are focused in one direction—toward Jesus. That's what a renewed mind will produce.

PART
Three

The Spirit of
Dissatisfaction

THE SPIRIT OF dissatisfaction is at war with the Holy
Spirit's efforts to renew our minds. Some people find it
difficult to live beyond yesterday because their hearts
are full of dissatisfaction. Sometimes dissatisfaction with
what we have and who we are leads us to seek satisfaction in yesterday. We wallow in the same emotions, music
or friendships that gave us what felt like satisfaction
when we were carnally minded. Worse yet, dissatisfaction may open the door for us to be tempted by any
number of sins. I believe that temptation is not possible
without dissatisfaction. When a man is satisfied with his
job, his family and his church, it is much more difficult
to tempt him away from that, no matter how attractive
the alternative. In the glow of satisfaction, other entice-
ments seem silly and uninviting.

Yet dissatisfaction plagues many people, and we ought
not underestimate its power. If dissatisfaction can affect
the perfect person in the perfect environment, as it did
Adam and Eve, we need to treat it seriously.

Eve's Dissatisfaction

Look for a minute at the first example of dissatisfaction in the entire human race. In 2 Corinthians 11, Paul says, "I am jealous for you with godly jealousy . . . But I fear, lest somehow, as *the serpent deceived Eve* by his craftiness, so your minds may be corrupted from the simplicity that is in Christ" (vv. 2–3, emphasis mine).

How did the serpent beguile or trick Eve? He was faced with a monumental task: to cause the perfect person in the perfect world to miss God. You can't tempt her with money—she has everything she needs. You can't tempt her with sex—she is married to the only other human being. Satan was trying to get Adam and Eve into the fallen condition he was in, and to do so he had to employ a series of crafty tricks that he still uses today to trip up and deceive Christians. Each of these steps led toward an ultimate goal: a dissatisfied heart that embraced sin. Watch how it happened.

First, Satan disguised himself in a spiritual conversation. Not all people who act spiritual have godly things in mind. There is a spiritual practice and speech that does not lead to victory or to your destiny. It's called by some "dead religion," and it is devoid of revelation. It may have the appearance of wisdom or cleverness, but it lacks the anointing of God. Have you ever caught yourself in a conversation with a fellow Christian and thought, *This doesn't seem to be going anywhere healthy?* Or have you been approached by someone and engaged in talk that sort of made you squirm on the inside, even though this person seemed very spiritual? It may have been that, though the words seemed spiritual, they were not of God.

This was certainly the case with Eve. Satan disguised his motives in words that were meant to give her the impression that he was knowledgeable and spiritual.

156

Second, he removed her from her covering: her husband. There is an order of authority in the kingdom of God, and in the marriage relationship, headship has been given to the man. As we all know, this does not make men superior. It is simply a kingdom principle God has laid down for our own good, and if we ignore it, we do so at our own peril.

Eve not only left the covering of her husband, but she was also isolated from his counsel. It is common knowledge that an isolated person is easier to defeat than a group of people. Tigers and other beasts of prey practice this principle when they chase herds of antelope or buffalo, separating one animal from the rest before pouncing on it. Authoritarian political regimes do the same thing when they prohibit people from meeting together for certain kinds of events or rallies.

Third, Satan used words to drive home the deception. He still uses words—counterfeit words that may sound persuasive but have no truth in them. It's interesting how the devil tries to use God's tools against Him. God created everything with a true Word, the Word made flesh. The devil tries to pollute and counteract the true Word with a false one. His words echo in people's minds all around the world. He knows that people are persuaded by words, that he can argue some people away from God with a sweet-sounding logic. That was his tactic then, and it remains his tactic to this day.

Finally, Satan was ready to go for humanity's jugular. His weapon: dissatisfaction. He created in Eve's mind the illusion of being dissatisfied with her current level of blessing. His words were meant to make her position seem inferior, trivial, unsatisfactory. He stirred up a self-centeredness in her that was disguised as self-help. He made her believe that God was holding out on her and Adam, and that if they ate of the forbidden fruit, they would be at His spiritual level. Think of it: He caused her to be dissatisfied with a thousand other trees and focus on only one, and that was enough leverage for him to throw all of mankind off course.

When Revelation Is Blocked

Eve could only be tempted after she had lost her satisfaction. She and her husband lost their privileged place in the Garden. They lost the opportunity to walk with God in a way that was uniquely possible in a sinless world. And, in a sense, humanity's revelation of God has grown steadily dimmer since that moment.

The most damaging thing about dissatisfaction is that it blocks revelation knowledge. Dissatisfaction keeps us from understanding God's purpose. It clouds our minds with selfish notions.

> *Dissatisfaction keeps us from understanding God's purpose. It clouds our minds with selfish notions.*

Revelation knowledge makes men stand strong. The lack of revelation knowledge drives men to come up with their own philosophies, traditions and wisdom. Without revelation, men are perpetually dissatisfied because they have no understanding; their eyes are blinded.

Revelation knowledge is God's answer for humanism and intellectualism. Men build up philosophies that are contrary to faith, but God's revelation knocks them down. Revelation knowledge keeps us close to God; it fills the hunger in the soul of man to know what is beyond his own mind. By revelation knowledge, God will speak to you and cause you to understand things that will spur you to righteousness and right living.

One of the most basic revelations that God helps us to understand is who we are in Christ. I've learned that men cannot stand any stronger than their revelation of who they are in Christ. The only way that you are going to be strong in the Lord is to have a revelation of who He is and who you are in Him. Paul said, "God willed to make known . . . this mystery . . . which is Christ in you, the hope of glory" (Col. 1:27). The mystery is revealed—Christ in you, the hope of glory. Paul declared that this fact was the foundation of all his revelation knowledge. The anointed One of God, Jesus the Messiah, now lives in earthen vessels. Christ in you— the hope, the divine expectation of the manifestation of the presence of God. If Jesus is not in you, then you have no right to expect that God is going to manifest Himself for you. But when you begin to understand the great mystery, Christ in you, the hope of glory, you suddenly get strong. Revelation knowledge gives you strength. It keeps you from being diverted from your destiny.

The only way you are going to be strong in the Spirit, Ephesians 3 says, is if you understand the anointing of God that resides in you. *Christ lives in you.* This revelation must be apprehended day by day, because if we are dissatisfied, the truth of it will grow dim in our eyes. When the devil tries to dissuade you, you are empowered by your revelation knowledge to say, "Devil, you're not challenging me alone—you're challenging me *and Christ in me.*" There's no such thing as fighting the devil alone when you get in the body of Christ.

The Disciples' Dissatisfaction

In John 14 we see that dissatisfaction blocked revelation knowledge and kept the disciples from understanding what Jesus told them and even who He was. For three years He had been telling them that He would die and rise again. Fourteen times Jesus spoke about His death. Eight times He spoke about His resurrection. That means the disciples heard Him talk about it at least twenty-two different times. He spent three and a half years training these twelve men to understand that He was going to die and come back from the dead.

"Let not your heart be troubled," Jesus told them in John 14:1–4. "You believe in God, believe also in Me. In My Father's house are many mansions; if it were not so I would have told you. I go to prepare a place for you. And if I go and prepare a place for you I will come again and receive you to Myself; that where I am, there you may be also. And where I go you know."

Then Thomas spoke up. "Lord, we do not know where You are going, and how can we know the way?" (v. 5).

So Jesus went back to Christianity 101. "I am the way, the truth, and the life. No one comes to the Father except through Me" (v. 6).

Philip said, "Lord, show us the Father, and it is sufficient for us" (v. 8).

It must have been disheartening to hear these words. Jesus had taught them twenty-two lessons on what would happen. Why didn't it sink in? Dissatisfaction had stopped revelation.

Think back for a moment on a few events that show what was in the disciples' hearts. They fought over who would sit on His right and left hands. They shoved the children away from Jesus. On one occasion, Peter was exasperated when Jesus wanted to feed the five thousand. Maybe things weren't moving along fast enough for them. Maybe they wanted a natural kingdom. Maybe they wanted privilege, access, status, a big bank account. Maybe they were dissatisfied with what Jesus was giving to them because it wasn't the flashy kind of kingdom or power they wanted.

Philip said, "Show us Him, and we will be satisfied." I contend that if Jesus would have shown the Father—if the Father would have stood right beside Him—they still would have found a way to be dissatisfied after the emotion of the moment was over. You don't think so? Consider the time Jesus took Peter, James and John up to the mountain, and God's voice spoke; the glory of God came, and Moses and Elijah appeared. When it was over they still abandoned Him a few days later. Why? Because they had seeds of dissatisfaction in their hearts.

We must learn to be content in all things. Paul said that he finally learned how to be content in whatever state he was in, whether abounding or abasing. (See Philippians 4:11.) He had made a decision that no one could steal his satisfaction and contentment. It's a spiritual truth that has to be learned, or we will fall into the same trap as the disciples did. If you are dissatisfied with your job, kids, marriage or even the preacher, it will block revelation knowledge. You must have a spirit of satisfaction.

Last year the Spirit of God spoke word of understanding to me that changed my life—because I obeyed it. The Spirit of the Lord said to me, "You must not let contentious people have access to your life if you are going to do what I tell you to do in the next phase of your ministry." I wrote it down and committed it to memory. I made a decision to cut ties in some areas. I re-ordered my life in obedience to God, and it was wonderful what happened after that in a short period of time. That doesn't mean that we don't minister to contentious people. We love everybody, and I will talk with anybody. But I will no longer allow contentious people to have ongoing access to my life. The spirit of contention, which springs from a spirit of dissatisfaction, is a thief that divides people and renders their prayers ineffective. There is tremendous power in agreement, and a tremendous lack of power in disagreement. Contention destroys the multiplied and the manifold power of God in our lives.

There will be times in your life when men and women will come into your church or your life and start fighting because they are dissatisfied. Let me tell you in advance, you don't need to fall in line with their dissatisfaction. You need to allow the satisfaction and contentment that's in you to heal them.

Godly Jealousy

If I could give you one piece of advice about avoiding dissatisfaction, it is this: Develop a godly jealousy over your satisfaction. Let no one rob you of it. Being satisfied is a learned, kingdom art. Once spiritual satisfaction is a part of you from the time you get up in the morning until the time you go to bed at night, then a jealousy—not a carnal jealousy, but a godly jealousy—will come over you, and anything that threatens to steal your satisfaction will be quickly rebuffed.

> *Develop a godly jealousy over your satisfaction. Let no one rob you of it.*

We need to learn to be jealous over one another with a godly jealousy. We have been so blessed with that ability at my church. In thirteen years we have never had a church split—and we never will by grace in Jesus' name. One of the reasons is because we love the people in front, behind and all around us. There is a godly jealousy for our relationship.

In 2 Corinthians 11 Paul wrote, "Oh, that you would bear with me in a little folly—and indeed you do bear with me. For I am jealous for you with godly jealousy.

For I have betrothed you to one husband, that I may present you as a chaste virgin to Christ" (vv. 1-2). The Lord began to deal with my heart about this one day, and I started weeping and crying uncontrollably. The revelation of God broke forth in my spirit so strongly that it literally overwhelmed me, and I could not go on. The Holy Spirit began to talk to my heart about the love of God. He spoke of how the church of the Lord Jesus Christ has lost the art of godly jealousy over our satisfaction and our relationships.

At one point in my life, I was jealous over my wife. She never gave me a reason to be jealous, but I was. But I have grown in the Lord, and now, after twenty-four years I am not jealous in a carnal sense. But I do have a godly jealousy. I have decided that what God has given me, I'm not giving up. I'm not letting go.

There is a godly jealousy in me that says I will not let anything steal the spirit of satisfaction from me again. I'm satisfied with what God is doing in my life right now. I know He has so much more, and I fully expect it to come; I am eager for it. But I am satisfied right now, and I fully anticipate being satisfied tomorrow.

You should get that in your spirit, too. It makes no difference how much money you have in the bank. It makes no difference how you feel. It makes no difference what you have to do today or don't have to do today—do yourself a favor and be satisfied. Let revelation knowledge flow readily to you and liberate you from your past. You won't be sorry you did. In fact, you'll be totally satisfied.

Chapter 11

The Bondage of Unforgiveness

I USED TO think that my enemies were my problem. Then I found out they're one of the keys to my promotion. I just have to be willing to act like Jesus toward them. Early one morning, the Holy Spirit spoke to me. He said, "You're about to enter into a season of mass recovery. People have hurt you, and because of what they have done they are now suffering. The devil is exacting a toll on their own lives. For every one of them that you help to recover, I will give you jubilee."

You cannot begin to live beyond yesterday if you won't forgive what happened yesterday. In my opinion, unforgiveness is the number one hindrance to living beyond yesterday. Forgiving others is one of the most powerful things we can do. It actually allows us to emulate how Jesus forgave us and to multiply that grace to others. You say, "But I don't want to do that. I just want to shoot them and send them on to heaven." The problem with that is, if you retain that person's offense, then it is retained to you. That's what Jesus said. But if you forgive

FROM THIS DAY ON . . .

them, it is now remitted to them. Every time someone offends you, even though you were innocent, the penalty of that is retained to you—unless you forgive them. But if you forgive them, it's all in their court, and you are free and clear to keep going forward in Christ.

Moses' Problem

Although most of us are familiar with the life of Moses, I discovered a few surprises when I began to study his life in detail. He was never supposed to have killed that Egyptian. He was never supposed to go to the back side of that mountain and live like a shepherd for forty years. Moses was trained in the house of Pharaoh to become the next Pharaoh. Pharaoh's own daughter raised him. God was raising him up to sit on that throne and lead the children of Israel out. But Moses missed it because of his own character defects, which perhaps had been in him from the time he was a little boy.

> *Unforgiveness is the number one hindrance to living beyond yesterday.*

I wonder if Moses didn't feel abandoned by his own parents, stuck in a basket of some kind and floated down the river. All of his brothers worked like slaves, dying like flies in the desert. I believe he was torn between two identities, his Egyptian training and his Hebrew roots, and this produced a bitterness in him. So when he saw a Hebrew and an Egyptian in a fight, his anger and unforgiveness boiled over, and the internal struggle became an external struggle—more precisely, a murder. Then, out of fear of Pharaoh, he took off running.

That's exactly the point where a lot of people are.

They have problems on the inside, and they lash out at others instead of being led by God. God came to Moses forty years later and continued the work, but that bitterness still cost him later. Moses smote the rock in a moment of anger, costing himself a trip to the Promised Land. Finally God hooked a Hebrew slave up to him who did not have that characteristic—a man without guile by the name of Joshua. When Moses would not change, he died, and Joshua wound up taking his place. There is no record anywhere in the Word that Joshua ever defied God. Yes, Moses was the most humble man who ever lived up to that point, as the Bible says, but he also had bitterness inside of him.

One of the men who prayed with me about beginning the church I pastor was one of the finest men I have known. He had more integrity than any man I've ever met. If he said something he did it. I believe that's how we ought to live. He loved God and was full of the Word. We traveled together and preached together. But he was just a young man when he died of cancer.

I'll never forget when he called me and told me that he had cancer. I said, "I know Jesus heals, and you do, too. I'll stand with you. I'm with you all the way." Yet, in no time the cancer spread, and he died.

I could not understand why he wasn't healed. In my grief I cried out to God, "God, You are going to have to help me on this thing." The Holy Spirit told me that my friend had a root of bitterness. He would not let it go, and it was a poison in him. He died because he wouldn't let it go.

His death was very hard for me. I watched him die over the course of several long months. Though he had cancer himself, he laid hands on people with cancer, and they were healed. He had great faith.

There was a certain offense that he had taken up in his life. It was a bitterness in his life. I knew exactly what it was, and I had talked to him about it. I had told him, "Get it out of you; get rid of it. Get healed from it, and let it go. It's not important." I advised him to forget the people who had wronged him, to release them and let the offense go. "You don't owe them anything," I said, "and they don't owe you anything."

My friend gave me his justifications for his feelings. It's important to know that even if you are right—even if you were truly wronged by another person—you can still let go of that offense. You don't have to try to get everybody else to believe your point, especially if it's a personal thing. If you're right, big deal, you're right—so what? Is the world going to stop? Is the sun going to stand still? Don't let that offense control your life. Don't feel as if you have to prove to everyone that you were right and the other person was wrong.

My friend's offense had become a bitterness in him. Every time we talked, before long the conversation cycled back to his feelings about that offense. The bitterness began to be evident in his words and actions.

When God revealed that fact to me, I don't mind telling you that I got on my knees and repented of everything I could think of in my life that could create any bitterness whatsoever. I let every offense and every person I could remember who had wronged me go. Just to be sure I had all my bases covered, I let some wrongs go that I knew I'd already let go earlier!

The Bible says, ". . . lest any root of bitterness springing up cause trouble, and by this many become defiled" (Heb. 12:15). The Greek would say, "Germinate. It begins to germinate and progress." God said that a root of bitterness is not just a spiritual thing. It can be a physical thing. Bitterness produces the fruit of the root. The word for *bitterness* is almost the same word as the word used for *acid* in the Greek.

I'm convinced that Moses had bitterness in him although

he was a meek man toward God. There was bitterness in him. He proved it over and over. It started from the time he was a little boy. Every time he tried to obey God, he was rejected and his motives were misjudged. Even when his motives were right, he still was misjudged. It no doubt hurt him badly. Moses had a very difficult time obeying God later on—especially when he was under pressure.

Moses died prematurely before he entered into the Promised Land. You may say, "Oh, but he was one hundred twenty years old." Yes, but he should have walked into that Promised Land with the rest of the Israelites.

Just as God put Barnabas, a man of great encouragement, together with Saul of Tarsus, so God put Joshua in the life of Moses. I believe He did it as much for the effect Joshua would have on Moses' life as He did it for the effect Moses would have on Joshua's life. Scripture doesn't tell us if Moses ever got his part out of that relationship, but Joshua got his. He became the leader who took Moses' place on that walk into the Promised Land.

Hebrews 12:14 says, "Pursue peace with all people." The Greek says, "Eagerly pursue peace with all men." Notice that the Bible says that you are going to have to pursue it. Peace doesn't come naturally. Many times the only thing that produces peace is war. Peace always comes after war. But peace has to be first pursued.

That's why I appreciate people who are willing to negotiate. Peace needs a strong defense. Every peace treaty is signed on a table of negotiation, not on a battlefield. I am a Vietnam veteran. I'm an honorable veteran, red, white and blue and all that stuff. But Vietnam could have been settled a long time before it was settled. Korea could have been settled a long time before we lost thousands of men. World War II could have been settled before it did, but the world pursued peace until the war ceased. Spiritually speaking, we must pursue peace with all men.

One of the main reasons people continue to dwell on the past is because they have not forgiven themselves. They can forgive others, but not themselves. In the Book of Hebrews, God said:

> Their sins and their lawless deeds I will remember *no more*.
> —HEBREWS 10:17, EMPHASIS ADDED

Not forgiving themselves for past sins is the main reason Christians do not walk in joy. If God does not hold you guilty of your past after you repent, then you are no longer guilty. We must learn the principle in the Word of forgiving ourselves and loosing that unforgiveness, or we will never be able to forget the former things.

> *You may be controlled today by the planting of yesterday, but you can control tomorrow by what you plant today.*

The Bible says, "I, even I, am He who blots out your transgressions for My own sake; and I will not remember your sins" (Isa. 43:25). God blotted out your transgressions for His sake. He forgave you when Jesus came to earth two thousand years ago and shed His blood on Calvary. So the forgiveness issue has been taken care of completely by Jesus Christ. Many people, however, are under the deception that they did something so bad that not even God can forgive them. My friend, if God would not receive you, then the work of Jesus on the cross would be entirely in vain.

One of the best ways to be delivered from the compulsions that control your life is to forgive yourself. God will put a new spirit in you—a supernatural spirit—and you will have the ability to forgive yourself. Wherever you are today, you are a product of what you have sown, or planted, in the past. If you have planted the wrong kinds of seeds—if you have not obeyed God and have not lived according to the Word of God or planted righteously— then you are reaping the fruit of what you have sown.

If, however, you begin to plant new seeds, you will reap an entirely new, godly product. You may be controlled today by the planting of yesterday, but you can control tomorrow by what you plant today.

Chapter 12

Depression–
Beauty for Ashes

A GREAT MANY people today remain bound in their minds with the spirit of mourning and depression—even though they have been saved and filled with the Holy Spirit. These people continue to experience a deep sense of grief and mourning over things that happened yesterday, a week ago, a month ago, a year ago, ten years ago, three marriages ago or four children ago. Depression can be one of the strongest echoes emanating from our past, and it can keep us from living beyond yesterday. I am sure that some of you reading this book are all too familiar with it.

Any time you step away from yesterday and begin living for what God is doing today, old bondages like depression will certainly come back and try to find a place in your life. Some of us deal with depression more than others, but I think all of us have to face it at one time or another.

A Mass Depression

According to Isaiah 61:3, those in Zion (Christians) can actually mourn. God's people can experience deep hurt; they can have heavy hearts and minds. Although their whole future is in front of them, people who mourn cannot feel hopeful or excited about it.

However, in the same passage, Jesus promises to comfort all those who mourn by giving them beauty for ashes.

> The Spirit of the Lord GOD is upon Me, because the LORD has anointed Me . . . to comfort all who mourn, to console those who mourn in Zion, to give them beauty for ashes, the oil of joy for mourning, the garment of praise for the spirit of heaviness.
>
> —ISAIAH 61:1–3

Ashes are associated with mourning or, as we refer to it in this generation, with depression. Apparently Jesus came across many people who were depressed in His day.

Depression can be one of the strongest echoes emanating from our past, and it can keep us from living beyond yesterday.

Imagine for a moment what it must have been like to be alive in Jesus' day. Most people had to walk everywhere they went. If a man was blessed to own a donkey or camel, he could explore a little farther. But since most people had to walk, they rarely traveled farther than twenty or thirty miles from their hometowns.

Because they had no outlet for finding satisfaction and

fulfillment of the "bigness" in their spirits, the people of Israel often felt enclosed. They spent their whole lives living inside little, boxlike houses made of mud bricks. Most of the houses looked exactly alike. In a way, these homes represented the emotions of the people who lived there—small and confined. That's how the Jewish people felt on the inside.

Because the Jews were oppressed for centuries, their dreams and ambitions were never allowed to flourish. All they could do was work to eat. Their world closed in on them, and they lived under the hard yokes of oppression that had been placed on them—both by their oppressors and by the oppression they felt by trying to satisfy all the requirements of the Law. They were a hurting people.

Can you imagine the emotions of men and women under those conditions? I am convinced that many of these people were depressed.

Then Jesus came. He began to say things like, "The Spirit of the LORD is upon Me, because He has anointed Me . . . to heal the brokenhearted, to proclaim liberty to the captives . . . to set at liberty those who are oppressed" (Luke 4:18). He was speaking straight into the heart of every person in Jerusalem when He spoke those things. His society was experiencing a mass depression. Everything was gray and downcast, as if the landscape and the people had been covered with a thin film of ashes.

Jesus knew that from time to time men and women would fight battles in their minds. As He Himself stated in Isaiah 61, Jesus offered the people of His day—and ours—soulish and spiritual liberty for those who were bound in their minds.

When Jesus comes into your heart and you get a revelation of His true power and anointing, you'll lose that appearance of ashes. You will begin to see everything in living color. I have often heard people say that after they got saved the trees looked greener and the sky looked twice as big and blue. That's because God had lifted the veil off their minds and hearts. When the veil is lifted, individuals go from being focused selfishly on their own small worlds to seeing themselves as part of God's plan. They become open to the purposes of God. Jesus said, "There is an anointing upon Me to reveal the truth to men and women, to console those who mourn in Zion, to give them beauty for ashes." (See Isaiah 61:3.)

An Ashes Mentality

Ashes are produced by something that has been burned black or charred. If you roast marshmallows and hot dogs over bright, blazing flames, you will eventually eat your fill and walk away from the fire. Pretty soon, after you stop adding fresh wood or charcoal briquettes, you will notice that the fire begins to die down and starts to go out. Finally, the fire reaches the point where it is nothing but a heap of smoldering ashes. You can stir the ashes, but you'll discover that the smoldering remains will produce no more flames. All that's left are gray, charred, smoldering ashes.

That's what happens to the souls of those who are in mourning. They have an ashes mentality. Nothing looks pretty. Do you know people like that? Everything just looks gray, because there is a spirit of heaviness upon them. They look at their spouses and think they look ugly. They look at their jobs, and even though they're making six-figure incomes a year, that job looks ugly. The car they bought yesterday is suddenly a piece of junk. It may be the most beautiful day of the year outside, but they can't see it. Why? Because they're depressed. All they can see is gray.

176

Jesus said, "I am anointed to give you beauty for ashes." When the anointing of God comes upon you, the Spirit of God will begin to open your eyes to the beauty around you that has been hidden from view. One of the first things you will experience is beauty in exchange for your ashes.

Sometimes circumstances in the lives and minds of men and women cause them to become burned out. Often there are unrealized goals, dreams, ambitions and even great calls of God that have become burned to the point that they are no longer recognizable.

The devil tries to put his fire—the fire of hurt, adversity and mourning—on the people of God. Many people are molded by this kind of fire. His goal is to reduce a person to a pile of ashes, then he can control that person with an ashes mentality. To someone with an ashes mentality, everything will appear flawed and ugly. That person will see no hope for tomorrow and no point to the future; even their countenance takes on a dreary appearance.

A Different Outlook

I've noticed that people who have just been filled with the Holy Spirit are always pushing toward tomorrow— toward the mark for the prize of the high calling of God in Christ Jesus (Phil. 3:14). They look around them and are thankful. They see things entirely different than the depressed person. The depressed person sees thirty-four degrees and drizzling rain as gloomy, but the person who has beauty in his eyes and heart will be able to say, "Bless God, this is the best duck weather I've ever seen."

The husband who receives beauty for ashes comes home from work and says something nice to his wife, even if the house is a mess. When God's beauty treatment is applied to your ashes mentality, the dreary job you've had for sixteen years will seem like a blessing, and you'll thank God for the income. In the radiance of God's beauty, those kids who seemed to be doing nothing but eating you out of house and home will seem like blessings.

The Book of Revelation tells us that God makes all things new. That's what happens when you receive beauty for ashes; the burned-out part of you is exchanged for God's beauty. When you make the decision to invite Jesus into your heart and ask Him to fill you with His Holy Spirit, depression will lift off of you. The echoes of the past will quiet down. Why? Because you are challenging the ash heap of your depression with the Word of God. When a person is in bondage to the spirit of mourning, his deliverance is not in Valium, a needle or something to drink, but in declaring the Word of God by the Spirit of God.

> *When a person is in bondage to the spirit of mourning, his deliverance is not in Valium, a needle or something to drink, but in declaring the Word of God by the Spirit of God.*

> And I will give you the keys of the kingdom of heaven, and whatever you bind on earth will be bound in heaven, and whatever you loose on earth will be loosed in heaven.
>
> —MATTHEW 16:19

Today you can be loosed from the ashes of depression, the spirit of mourning.

The Oil of Joy for Mourning

I love cars. Sometimes my wife, Cindy, and I will stop off at a car lot so I can look at them. I once had a nice Mercury Monterey that had a slow oil leak. I was unaware of this leak because I didn't pay much attention to the car. One night I tried to jump-start a friend's battery from my car. After repeatedly revving up the engine, it threw a rod right through the block. I learned from that experience that a car will run for a little while without oil, but eventually the engine will either freeze up or blow up.

People are like that, too. When they run out of oil in their spirits, they get into a state of mourning, as if they're grinding metal on metal.

Human beings are living machines. In order to operate properly, we need more than blood coursing through our veins. There is an ingredient that runs much deeper than blood. It's called joy. Joy flows from our spirits, and it is as important to human beings as blood.

You'll remember that in previous chapters we talked about how Jesus grew strong in His spirit, a trait I associate directly with joy. Joy is more than laughter and merriment, though it is that. Joy is a rich combination of assurance, hope, anticipation and a deep, abiding peace.

The devil tries to offer counterfeits for joy. He will tempt you with all types of deviations such as drugs and alcohol to use in your attempt to be rid of the pain of depression. He may lead you into excesses in some areas, like work or eating. These things make matters worse. After the desires of the flesh are satisfied, you will have the added problem of guilt.

The workaholic, the alcoholic, the overeater and the drug user are all running around in circles, revving up their engines without any joy to lubricate their motors. All the devil can ever offer is a cheap counterfeit that ultimately will bind you up and leave you in bondage, causing a worse problem than the one you had originally.

Oil Under Pressure

But God promises to give us the oil of joy for mourning (Isa. 61). One of the mightiest ministries of the Spirit of God is to administer the oil of joy. I don't know about you, but I can use a little oil of the Spirit, especially when I'm under pressure. I have found that during times of pressure, the oil of the Spirit—the oil of joy—works better than at any other time. It's like making orange juice. When you squeeze the orange, instead of ruining the orange, you get orange juice. The more you squeeze, the more orange juice you get. When you receive the oil of joy while under pressure, other people will see only the oil. You will radiate God's joy even in the midst of mourning.

> *Joy flows from our spirits, and it is as important to human beings as blood.*

Whenever you're hurting or experiencing problems, refuse to give in to the problems. The more pressure that comes on you, the more capacity you have to "joy in the Lord" and rejoice in the joy of your salvation.

There is only one way to receive the oil of joy for mourning, and that is by the Spirit of God. Only the Lord can give it to you. When you receive the oil of joy for mourning, all those heated-up emotions, along with the depression and hurt, will begin to subside.

When Jesus told the parable of the good Samaritan, He revealed that this good traveler used both oil and wine to help the wounded beggar he found by the roadside. (See Luke 10:25–37.) This parable foreshadowed events in the Book of Acts, where the apostles and disciples of that day administered the oil and wine. In both the Old and New Testaments, oil represents the Holy Spirit.

In the New Testament, oil represents the new birth, and wine represents the baptism of the Holy Spirit. People who received this new "wine" began to speak in other tongues and to dance and rejoice. Many who saw them thought they were drunk, but they were simply filled with new wine. What was the wine? It was the wine of the Spirit. The people who had been oppressed received the oil of joy for mourning. This same wine— the oil of joy—is still available today.

The Necessity of Oil

When my Mercury Monterey blew up, I learned that a mechanical or electrical engine will not run for an extended period of time without oil. You may have a brand-new engine in your car, but if there is an oil leak, you will drive down the road without even realizing you're in trouble. But after you've driven a while with that slow leak, the engine will be rubbing metal on metal. There will be nothing to lubricate all the internal parts of the engine except a thin film of oil residue. When that residue breaks down, the motor will start to cut out, and then you'll be stuck.

In the same way, you have to keep your spiritual and mental engine running properly. Why do we say that joy is the lubricant of the Spirit? Because it oils your soul. If you can learn to rejoice in the God of your salvation, you will discover that the kingdom of God will come to life within you. And it will be glorious.

> Rejoice in the Lord always. Again I will say, rejoice!
> —Philippians 4:4

When you learn to rejoice in the Lord, you will discover the although you may not experience joy for all things, you can experience joy *always.*

People who are caught up in depression, compulsive behavior patterns and ungodly lifestyles are almost always occupied with thoughts of yesterday. A song or conversation may trigger a memory, but you must be willing to shut out those echoes.

> Do not remember the former things, nor consider the things of old.
> —Isaiah 43:18

If you allow yourself to sit around and dwell on how things used to be—whether negative or positive—the past will literally captivate your mind. It will keep you from serving God and will control your future, because you are the sum total of what you think about and what you say. Before long, thoughts about the past will completely engulf you and choke out the newness of the life of God in you.

Paul and Silas

From Bible accounts, we know that Paul was a rather straightforward individual. As Saul of Tarsus, he killed Christians. Once gloriously transformed and filled with the Holy Spirit, Paul was a dynamo for God.

Paul was thrown into prison for his Christian teachings.

Silas, who traveled with Paul on his first evangelistic trip, was imprisoned with him. Can you picture them in jail? Whipped and thrown into the lower prison, their hands and feet were placed in painful stocks. Who knows what thoughts of depression they had to fight off—but they did it. Even in the depths of a Roman jail, these two great men of God found a reason and a way to rejoice.

Paul and Silas weren't happy about being in jail; but they had the oil of joy for mourning. The Holy Spirit had equipped and anointed them to rejoice despite the fact that they had reason to mourn. They began to sing songs, hymns and spiritual songs in the midst of the prison at midnight, and God sent an earthquake to set them free.

Paul and Silas decided to rejoice in the God of their salvation. Rejoicing in one's salvation does not just mean rejoicing over the fact that one is born again. There are seven different meanings for the term *salvation,* and one of them is "total deliverance." When you begin to rejoice in the God of your salvation, you too can receive total deliverance.

We don't have to surrender to mourning—we have oil—but we do have to keep right on swimming through that thing that surrounds us and threatens to overtake us.

I once heard a story about two frogs that fell into a butter churn filled with milk. At first, they just swam around. After a while, they began to tire. One frog decided to be depressed and quit—and he sank to the bottom and drowned. The other frog was determined not to go down and wouldn't give up. Pretty soon, as the milk began to thicken, he jumped onto an "island" of butter and soon jumped right out of the churn.

It's the same with you and me. God will give us the oil of joy for mourning. We don't have to surrender to mourning—we have oil—but we do have to keep right on swimming through that thing that surrounds us and threatens to overtake us. We have to keep on thanking God and shouting, "Hallelujah! God has delivered me."

God delivered Daniel out of the lions' den; Shadrach, Meshach and Abednego from the fiery furnace; David, Samson, Moses and many others from unfortunate circumstances. All these men had one thing in common: They didn't throw up their hands and quit. They kept right on swimming through their problems and received deliverance.

Acts 10:34 says that God is no respecter of persons. What He has done for a multitude of others, He will do for you. You cannot allow the devil to steal your joy, however. You have to keep right on swimming. When you do, the oil of joy within you will keep you from burning out. We are the lamps of this world. The only time a lamp can burn out is when it has run out of oil. God will give you the oil of joy for mourning.

The Garment of Praise for the Spirit of Heaviness

Heaviness is when you wake up in the morning and dread getting out of bed. Everything looks bleak—today, the future, your marriage, your lifestyle, your job—you have no hope. Some of you know exactly what I'm talking about.

Heaviness, my friend, is a spirit. It's one of the devil's chief tactics in defeating people. But the Word of God has a weapon for you. God says the Spirit of the Lord will issue you a garment of praise.

When a person is experiencing depression, it's like being in the midst of a desert. Everywhere you look there is sand, heat and dryness. When the children of God wandered in the wilderness for forty years, they were constantly surrounded by dryness and dangers. There was barrenness everywhere. But in the midst of their desert experience, God told them:

> Behold, I will do a new thing, now it shall spring forth; shall you not know it? I will even make a road in the wilderness and rivers in the desert.
>
> —ISAIAH 43:19

And that's what God did—He made a way for His children in the wilderness. He caused manna to rain down from heaven and water to spring forth from a rock.

Yes, God knows of many ways to bless you, but you must decide to receive those new things instead of dwelling on past things. Isaiah 43:20 says, "The beast of the field will honor Me, the jackals and the ostriches, because I give waters in the wilderness and rivers in the desert, to give drink to My people, My chosen." God is telling you that in the middle of your wilderness, He will give you something to drink because you are His chosen people.

There are many kinds of garments that a person can put on, but not every garment is appropriate for all occasions. The Bible says that God will supply a garment of praise for the spirit of heaviness. That is the right kind of garment for a depressed person to wear. You must choose to wear the garment of praise at all times. Say, "Bless God, I'm not going to wear that garment of depression any longer. I'm going to start praising God."

Can you imagine God saying, "I've never had such a bad day. I don't think I'll get out of bed tomorrow." What if Jesus had decided not to come down to the earth and give His life as a ransom for sinners because He didn't feel like it? No, God doesn't have bad days. He doesn't give in to His feelings. Jesus is not controlled by His emotions.

Ephesians 5:1 says, "Be imitators of God as dear children." We should imitate God, *as dear children.* In order to break the spirit of heaviness, you will have to put on the garment of praise and take off the garment of heaviness. You will need to make a conscious decision to imitate the thoughts, attitudes and feelings of God. In order to do that, you're going to have to rejoice.

> Do not be drunk with wine, in which is dissipation; but be filled with the Spirit, speaking to one another in psalms and hymns and spiritual songs, singing and making melody in your heart to the Lord.
>
> —EPHESIANS 5:18–19

When you rejoice, you will activate the anointing of the Holy Spirit—because the Spirit of God responds to the Word of God. As a result, heaviness will be lifted off of you.

Power in God's Word

The Word of God says, "Put Me in remembrance; let us contend together; state your case, that you may be acquitted" (Isa. 43:26). What does that mean? It means that you and I can remind God of what His Word says and of what He has done in the lives of men and women throughout history. What He has done for Moses, Abraham, Solomon, Paul and many others, He will also do for you and me.

When you begin to praise God and put Him in remembrance of His Word, that spirit of heaviness will lift off you. As new things begin to spring forth, stay close to the Word of God—no matter what happens, good or bad. If you're sad, rejoice; if you're hurting, rejoice; if you don't have enough money in the bank, rejoice. At all times, thank the Lord that He supplies all your need according to His riches in glory by Christ Jesus (Phil. 4:19).

When you begin to praise God and put Him in remembrance of His Word, that spirit of heaviness will lift off you.

Paul said, "I have learned in whatever state I am, to be content" (Phil. 4: 11). As you stay in the Word and speak the Word, you will stop dwelling on yesterday and start thinking God's way in the here and now.

Chapter 13

The Sound of an Abundance of Rain

You won't find anything about God that is less than enough in the Scriptures, nor will you find anything about God that is just enough in the Scriptures. What you find about God is abundance—more than enough. Today in my spirit I hear the sound of an abundance of rain. Before the rain can fall, someone has to hear it first, and then someone has to see it and voice it to others. When that takes place, everything changes. There is a sound of abundance coming right now in our land.

Living in a Land Without Rain

There is a story in the Bible that teaches us what it is like to live in a land without rain.

During the days of Elijah, Israel was not serving the Lord. The entire nation had followed the lead of a series of wicked kings who had led the nation into idolatry and wickedness. After the death of Omri, Ahab, his son, became king of Israel. Ahab was a very wicked king.

> Now Ahab the son of Omri did evil in the sight of
> the LORD, more than all who were before him. And it
> came to pass, as though it had been a trivial thing for
> him to walk in the sins of Jeroboam the son of Nebat,
> that he took as wife Jezebel the daughter of Ethbaal,
> king of the Sidonians; and he went and served Baal
> and worshiped him. Then he set up an altar for Baal
> in the temple of Baal, which he had built in Samaria.
> And Ahab made a wooden image. Ahab did more to
> provoke the LORD God of Israel to anger than all the
> kings of Israel who were before him.
>
> — 1 KINGS 16:30–33

Not only was Ahab a wicked king, but Jezebel, his wife,
was the high priestess of Baal and led the prophets of
Baal in their idolatry. She has been described as "a Sidonian
princess, an imperious, unscrupulous, vindictive, determined, devilish woman, a demon incarnate."* Baal was the
god of fertility, and the idolatrous doctrines of Baal had
permeated the nation of Israel. Sensuality and immorality
ran rampant. The doctrines of Baal had affected every part
of the nation's lifestyle—socially, politically, physically,
financially and spiritually. The Israelites, who had been
delivered by God from the slavery of Egypt, had entered
into slavery of the soul—into a godless philosophy that
had nothing to do with the personal, intimate relationship
with the living God that they had once experienced.

The doctrine of Baal was the doctrine of fertility. Baal
controlled even the rain. The crops were under the control of Baal. Baal was the reason that cows would calf,
sheep would bear lambs and mothers would give birth to
children. The people were obsessed by this wicked religion. They regularly crowded into the temples that had
been erected to this god, and there they made sacrifices
to Baal—sometimes sacrificing their own children. They
engaged in immoral sexual relationships with the wicked

prophets of Baal and with the temple prostitutes. They pleaded with Baal to bless their crops and guide their lives. They were completely bound emotionally under the grip of this wicked cult.

It was into this godless climate of idolatry that Elijah had been called by God to be a prophet. Elijah was God's answer to Ahab and Jezebel. God sent Elijah to eradicate the worship of Baal. He was courageous and full of fiery zeal for the living God. God gave Elijah power to shut the heavens for three and a half years.

> Elijah the Tishbite, of the inhabitants of Gilead, said to Ahab, "As the LORD God of Israel lives, before whom I stand, there shall not be dew nor rain these years, except at my word."
>
> — I KINGS 17:1

Do you know what happens when you live in an agricultural country like Israel, and because of a prophecy that you give, no rain falls for a period of three and a half years? Elijah, in essence, had control of that land. He controlled the economy of the land—which depended on rain to produce its crops. He controlled the farms, the finances, even the emotions of the land.

Elijah was a nobody who came from nowhere. Yet God raised him up to override the godless doctrines of Baal.

A modern-day example similar to what Israel experienced during these three and a half years is the country of Ethiopia. It doesn't rain for years at a stretch in that country, and all we have to do is take a look at the political, social, physical, financial and spiritual state of that nation to see what happens when the rain fails to fall.

A Nobody From Nowhere

Elijah was a nobody who came from nowhere. Yet God raised him up to override the godless doctrines of Baal. Elijah wasn't fearful about confronting the wicked philosophies of Baal. He had experienced an intimate and life-changing relationship with the living God—and it made all the difference in his life.

I believe that God is raising up Elijahs to confront the wickedness and vain philosophies of this generation today. God's people are beginning to rise up with boldness. Religion as usual isn't good enough anymore. God is pulling together a mighty army of Elijahs who have recognized the devastation of a world without rain — without the rain of the Holy Spirit and the revelations of a living God. This army cares nothing about the world's vain philosophies—they live in the awesome glory of a personal relationship with God and the mercy and grace that has been granted to them by Jesus, God's only Son.

God raised up Elijah to free His people from their soul slavery. The first thing Elijah did was to strike at the heart of Baal's domination. He walked into the throne room of wicked king Ahab and his demonized wife, Jezebel. As he stood before them, he threw the gauntlet down—he made a courageous stand for truth. He announced God's edict that no rain would fall for three and a half years. Then he said, "OK, Jezy; come on, Ahab, let's see what you can do about it!"

God's army of Elijahs is charging into the throne room of present-day kings and demons and declaring an end to their godless control over the people God wants for His own. They are declaring that you can't be immoral enough to make it rain. You can't get enough money to make things right between yourself and God. No man ever has or ever will.

The religious philosophies of today are as powerless as the godless doctrines of Baal. You can put on religious robes, follow religious rules, sponsor religious programs —but if the Holy Spirit isn't at work in your life, the rain isn't going to fall.

God is not historic; He is revelation. He is not a yesterday thought; He is a now voice, a today word.

Faith is not knowing what God did yesterday. Faith is a relationship with a living God. Jezebel didn't have one. Ahab didn't have one. But Elijah did.

When he heard God say it wasn't going to rain, it didn't rain; it dried up. When it dried up, the crops didn't grow. The money didn't flow. The cows didn't calf. The horses didn't foal. The sheep didn't have lambs.

That three and a half years must have been devastating for Ahab and Jezebel. Every day they were faced with the knowledge that one little old nobody—and his awesome God—had dealt them a mortal blow right in the center of the thing upon which they had banked their whole existence—and that of the Israelites. Elijah had confronted Baal, their god of fer-

> *God is not historic; He is revelation. He is not a yesterday thought; He is a now voice, a today word.*

tility, and in essence had said to him, "OK, big bad Baal, you claim to be the god of all fertility, let's see how fertile you are without rain."

And while Ahab and Jezebel and the entire nation

reeled under the blow from Elijah, withering into impotent has-beens, Elijah continued walking into a closer and more intimate relationship with the living God. And when those desperate years began to draw to a close, Elijah caught the sound of the abundance of rain. But it didn't come all at once. There were three important steps that Elijah had to take first.

Elijah Had to Hear the Sound of Rain

One day while Elijah was fellowshiping with his God, God spoke quietly to him. "Elijah," He whispered gently, "listen to what I'm letting you hear."

I can imagine Elijah cocking his head to one side, listening intently, and then responding to God, "What is it, God? All I hear is the rustling of dried, dead wheat blowing in the sunbaked creek bed that no longer gives me water. Or the flapping of the wings of the ravens as they fly overhead, no longer bringing me food. Or the low moaning of the cattle for water, and the bleating of the ewes for their dead lambs. But I've been hearing that for a long time now."

But God insisted that he listen again. He may have said the words that were later recorded in Mark 4:24: "Take heed what you hear. With the same measure you use, it will be measured to you; and you who hear, more will be given." Or perhaps God admonished Elijah as Jesus admonished His followers in Luke 8:18: "Therefore take heed how you hear. For whoever has, to him more will be given; and whoever does not have, even what he seems to have will be taken from him." God was teaching Elijah an important principle that the Elijahs of today need to learn. Be careful how you listen and what you hear. Because if you hear it wrong, what you have will be taken from you. But if you hear it right, even more than what you have will be given to you.

We must be willing to hear things the way God says them. In both of these verses, God said that if Elijah heard correctly, more would be given to him. But if he heard wrong, even what he had would be taken from him. Elijah would see that principle come to pass in just a few short days—both times through the faith of two women.

There are religious movements in this country that began years ago by men and women who heard the sound of the abundance of rain. But many of these movements have forgotten that sound and have moved away from their intimate relationship with the God of the sound of rain. They have theorized and philosophized themselves into dead or dying religious institutions and no longer know how to hear what God is saying. They hear only famine when God wanted them to hear abundance.

God didn't want Elijah—or His people in any generation after Elijah—to hear the sounds of famine and thirst. He wanted him to hear the sound of an abundance of rain. And once he heard that sound, God wanted Elijah to remember that sound until he took the second step— until he saw the abundance of rain.

Elijah Had to See the Abundance of Rain

One day as Elijah sat quietly listening to the sound of abundance of rain, God spoke again to him. "OK, Elijah, I've supplied enough sounds of rain for you to hear. Now it's time to go public with this thing. Here's what I want you to do. I want you to go down to Zarephath where you will meet a widow woman." We can read the account in 1 Kings 17:

> Then the word of the LORD came to him, saying, "Arise, go to Zarephath, which belongs to Sidon, and dwell there. See, I have commanded a widow there to provide for you." So he arose and went to

Zarephath. And when he came to the gate of the city, indeed a widow was there gathering sticks. And he called to her and said, "Please bring me a little water in a cup, that I may drink"

And as she was going to get it, he called to her and said, "Please bring me a morsel of bread in your hand." So she said, "As the LORD your God lives, I do not have bread, only a handful of flour in a bin, and a little oil in a jar; and see, I am gathering a couple of sticks that I may go in and prepare it for myself and my son, that we may eat it, and die."

— I KINGS 17:8–12

I can imagine that when God told Elijah that he would meet a widow woman who would care for him, Elijah may have thought it would be a rich widow with an abundance of food and water in spite of the famine in the land. But this widow was not rich. In fact, all her provisions were gone except enough flour and oil to prepare one last meal for herself and her son. She didn't hear the sound of the abundance of rain. She heard only the wailing of her starving son.

But when God allowed Elijah to hear the sound of rain he heard more than that. He heard the crops growing; he heard the tassels of full-grown corn rustling in the breezes and the money flowing back into the hands of the farmers. He heard the sound of calves drawing milk from their mothers and the lambs snuggling close to the sheep.

You see, he could hear what no one else could hear. He could hear the beginning of the move of the Holy Spirit.

And he had heard God say that this widow woman would care for him. She heard only the sound of the oil flowing out of her jar—but Elijah heard the sound of fresh oil flowing into the jar.

Elijah knew that in order for the sound of the abundance of rain to be heard by this widow woman, she would have to be willing to give what she had away. So he asked her to bring him a glass of water. It may have been the last water she had—but she had to give it to get more. The abundance of God always begins with what you do now.

That's a spiritual principle that is true in every circumstance. God sent His Son, Jesus, to pay the cost of our salvation. The price has been paid. Salvation—with its abundance of life eternal—is already ours. God wants the whole world to be saved. But just because He wants us saved doesn't mean that we are. We can only be saved by giving ourselves to Him and receiving His

> *The abundance of God always begins with what you do now.*

gift of salvation. It is not God's will that any should perish, but that all should come to repentance. But some are going to perish; not all are going to come to repentance. Just because God wants us to be blessed does not mean that we are blessed. Everything we receive from God works on the same principle.

God has mercy for every sinner. Mercy is God's sovereign gift to all. Through the death, burial and resurrection of Jesus, God's grace has been extended to every sinner. But faith is the hand that reaches into the bucket of grace and draws it back into the seen realm.

We see that faith in the widow at Zarephath. She began to hear the same sound of the abundance of rain as Elijah spoke to her. She stepped forward in her faith in that sound and gave what she had to get more. Let's take a look at her response:

> And Elijah said to her, "Do not fear; go and do as you have said, but make me a small cake from it first, and bring it to me; and afterward make some for yourself and your son. For thus says the LORD God of Israel: 'The bin of flour shall not be used up, nor shall the jar of oil run dry, until the day the LORD sends rain on the earth.'" So she went away and did according to the word of Elijah; and she and he and her household ate for many days. The bin of flour was not used up, nor did the jar of oil run dry, according to the word of the LORD which He spoke by Elijah.
>
> —1 KINGS 17:13–16

At first this woman had heard only the sounds of famine and death. Unwilling to give, she had almost talked herself out of three thousand meals. Faith comes by hearing. For some, faith leaves by hearing—hearing the wrong sounds. At first, she turned to walk away from Elijah, and almost walked away from the miracle that changed her nation and left a legacy for the Elijahs of today.

Elijah had to compel her to make a cake for him first. He knew that if she acted in faith and obeyed God, she would not die. But he didn't tell her that. He said only, "OK, make a last meal for you and your son if you want to, *but make a little cake for me first.*"

She responded in faith, and she and the prophet and her entire household ate for three years. Equate it any way you want; she traded a little piece of cake for three thousand meals.

I can imagine that the first time she went back to her jar and saw more oil, she began to hear what Elijah had heard. She began to see what Elijah was seeing. She began to hear and see an abundance of rain.

I hear the abundance of rain myself—right now. Like Elijah, I see the rain coming, and I long to see others step out in faith by giving what they have to receive that abundant rain in their lives. God wants to pour His rain upon you, upon your family, upon your church, your community—upon the world. But you must hear the sounds, and you must see that rain before it will begin to fall. And when you can see the rain, then it's time to get prepared for the miracle supply of the abundance of rain.

Elisha also met a woman who had heard and seen the promise of rain. (See 2 Kings 4:8-17.) She knew the importance of preparing for the miracle. She built a room for Elisha on the side of her house. She provided a place for a move of God in her own home.

Some people may never get a miracle until they make room for the move of God. It cost money for that woman to build a room for Elisha. But she was willing to give what she had to prepare for the abundance of rain.

When I built my house I remembered this important lesson from this woman. I built a room for my spiritual father, Lester Sumrall, in my home. I wanted a place for him to stay when he came in my direction. And now some of the greatest men and women of faith have

All miracles begin at the point of perception.

slept in my home. No wonder I have three blessed daughters. No wonder my wife has experienced the blessing of God in abundance.

That woman perceived that Elisha was a man of God. And when she did, the miracle began. All miracles begin at the point of perception. Either we see it or we don't. If we see it, we can have what we see. God blessed this woman for her perception. She and her husband had been unable to have a child before she built the room for Elijah. But when she stepped out in faith to give in order to receive what she saw, God blessed them with a child.

Elijah Had to Voice
the Abundance of Rain

Elijah had another step to take before the rain could begin to fall. He had heard the rain. He had seen the rain coming—and helped the widow to see it, too. Now he had to give voice to the news of impending rain. And this time, as he voiced the sound of the abundance of rain, the entire nation witnessed it—including Ahab and Jezebel. In one single day, Elijah and the living God stamped out the claims of Baal in a miraculous manifestation of God's power.

Elijah once again charged into Ahab's presence with a message from God:

> Then it happened, when Ahab saw Elijah, that Ahab said to him, "Is that you, O troubler of Israel?" And he answered, "I have not troubled Israel, but you and your father's house have, in that you have forsaken the commandments of the LORD and have followed the Baals. Now therefore, send and gather all Israel to me on Mount Carmel, the four hundred and fifty prophets of Baal, and the four hundred prophets of Asherah, who eat at Jezebel's table."
>
> —1 KINGS 18:17–19

I'm persuaded that Elijah had been hearing the abundance of rain for quite some time before he finally voiced it. There are men and women today who have been hearing in the spirit from God. Just as He told the servants in John, Jesus is telling His servants today to draw out the water. (See John 2:1-11.)

There comes a time when He says, "Draw out now." I

believe that word is being deposited in the spirits of the men and women of God who are hearing what God is saying. I hear Him saying that there is an abundance of rain coming. Draw out now! This is the time we are in right now. We have heard it; we have seen it; and now we have to voice it! Be willing to say it. I have found out that God will only fill you to the degree that you will open your mouth.

> *I have found out that God will only fill you to the degree that you will open your mouth.*

Once again Elijah gave a bold challenge to Baal— and to Jezebel and her prophets. In essence he was telling them that he had heard and seen the abundance of rain. Let's see how he voices this vision that had arisen in his spirit and now is being told to the entire nation:

> "I alone am left a prophet of the LORD; but Baal's prophets are four hundred and fifty men. Therefore let them give us two bulls; and let them choose one bull for themselves, cut it in pieces, and lay it on the wood, but put no fire under it; and I will prepare the other bull, and lay it on the wood, but put no fire under it. Then you call on the name of your gods, and I will call on the name of the LORD; and the God who answers by fire, He is God." . . . And so it was, at noon, that Elijah mocked them and said, "Cry aloud, for he is a god; either he is meditating, or he is busy, or he is on a journey, or perhaps he is sleeping and must be awakened." . . . And when midday was past, they prophesied until the time of the offering of the evening sacrifice.

But there was no voice; no one answered, no one paid attention....

And Elijah took twelve stones, according to the number of the tribes of the sons of Jacob....Then with the stones he built an altar in the name of the LORD; and he made a trench around the altar large enough to hold two seahs of seed. And he put the wood in order, cut the bull in pieces, and laid it on the wood, and said, "Fill four waterpots with water and pour it on the burnt sacrifice and on the wood." Then he said, "Do it a second time," and they did it a second time; and he said, "Do it a third time," and they did it a third time. So the water ran all around the altar; and he also filled the trench with water.

—1 KINGS 18:22–24, 27, 29, 31–35

The prophets of Baal had heard nothing from their god. They saw nothing—no demonstration of power, no response of any kind. Just an empty, death-charged silence.

But Elijah had heard and seen, and he was prepared for a miraculous intervention from the living God. He knew there was an abundance of rain about to fall. And with that rain would come the fiery presence of the God of Israel, the one true God in awesome power. Perhaps he poured the water on to signify the soon pouring on of the water of God. Perhaps he wanted them to hear the sound of floods of water. It's certain that he saw in that water something those 450 prophets of Baal could not see. He saw the floodgates of heaven opening and God coming forth in a magnificent display of power.

And it came to pass, at the time of the offering of the evening sacrifice, that Elijah the prophet came near and said, "LORD God of Abraham, Isaac, and Israel, let it be known this day that You are God in Israel and I am Your servant, and that I have done all these things at Your word. Hear me, O LORD, hear me, that this people may know that You are the LORD God, and that You have turned their hearts back to You again."

Then the fire of the LORD fell and consumed the burnt sacrifice, and the wood and the stones and the dust, and it licked up the water that was in the trench. Now when all the people saw it, they fell on their faces; and they said, "The LORD, He is God! The LORD, He is God!" And Elijah said to them, "Seize the prophets of Baal! Do not let one of them escape!" So they seized them; and Elijah brought them down to the Brook Kishon and executed them there.

Then Elijah said to Ahab, "Go up, eat and drink; for there is the sound of abundance of rain."

— 1 KINGS 18:36–41

Elijah could no longer keep silent! He spoke forth the vision of abundant rain that he had carried in his spirit for three and a half years. He said, "Get ready, it's going to start raining."

I have seen that same vision, and I cannot keep it silent. Get ready, it's going to start raining. I prophesy in the name of Jesus that there are people in this country who are going to get saturated with the rain of the Spirit. When I hear that rain falling, I don't just hear spiritual wisdom. I hear the blessing of finances, prosperity, abundance in healing, signs, wonders, miracles and provision.

Christ came to redeem us from the curse (Gal. 3:13). In the Greek language, the word *redeemed* is translated *exagorazo*. From that word we get the word *exaggerate*, which means "an excessive display, an excessive amount, an exaggeration, an embellishment."

> *If He dealt with the ultimate need in advance, up front, what makes you think He will withhold any of the lesser things that you need today?*

God hath redeemed us in a big way! Christ has *exagorazo*. I contend that one drop of His blood would have saved the souls of all the world. But Jesus bled all His blood and offered it on the altar of God. He did more than enough. Why do you think He would give you less than enough today, when He did more than enough in redemption for you? He redeemed you from all the curse of yesterday.

I like what it says in Romans 8:32:

> He who did not spare His own Son, but delivered Him up for us all, how shall He not with Him also *freely give us all things?*
>
> —EMPHASIS ADDED

If He dealt with the ultimate need in advance, up front, what makes you think He will withhold any of the lesser things that you need today?

I once heard a minister say that we need to get rid of our "skinny-goat mentality." The older brother of the prodigal son had a skinny-goat mentality. Upon the return of his younger brother, he came to his father, complaining, "Look! For so many years I have been serving you, and I have never neglected a command of yours; and yet you have never given me a kid [skinny goat], that I might be merry with my friends; but when this son of yours came, who has devoured your wealth with harlots, you killed the fattened calf for him." (See Luke 15:29–30.)

This son's skinny-goat mentality hindered him from seeing the abundance of rain. The father didn't have any skinny goats to kill for his sons. All he had were fattened calves for his people.

We've got to get rid of the skinny-goat mentality or it will make us a slave in the field when we're supposed to be heirs and joint heirs with the Father. That son had been slaving in the field because of his own mind. Any time you misjudge God, and you carry an offense toward the goodness of God, then you misjudge the benefits that are available to you. He misjudged the heart of the father—and he shortchanged himself.

Thank God, we don't have to live that way today. It makes no difference if you are a prince or a pauper. In Christ Jesus you can go where God wants you to go.

The Scripture says that Elijah said that there was the sound of abundance of rain. Abundance always begins with a sound in the Spirit.

How the Rain Appears

Be sure that you can hear the sound of God's abundant rain. Elijah heard it. But neither Ahab or Elijah's servant could hear the sound. Both the enemy and the ally can miss the voice of God. The one who hears is the one whose heart is open and who has an intimate relationship with the living God. There are many Christians whom I call allies of God who do not hear any more than Elijah's servant heard. And there are many enemies like Ahab who will never hear.

If we can hear and believe, we can have the abundance of rain.

The Bible says that Ahab went up to eat and to drink. But Elijah went to the top of Carmel, cast himself down upon the earth, put his face between his knees and began to pray. Every move of God is activated by prayer and intercession from men and women who have a revelation of what God is doing and saying. As Elijah interceded for the rain, he gave instructions to his servant:

> "Go up now, look toward the sea." So he went up and looked, and said, "There is nothing." And seven times he said, "Go again."
>
> — 1 KINGS 18:43

Elijah had to send his servant to look for rain seven times. "Why don't you just go and look until you can see what I can hear?" he told the servant. "Why don't you keep looking until you see what I hear in the spirit?"

The servant kept looking until he could see what could be heard. That's so important. People of faith always keep looking until they see what God has said. It may look negative and difficult all around, but they just keep looking.

There is a woman in the New Testament who kept looking for what she had heard and seen in the spirit. (See Mark 5:25–29.) She had been struggling with an issue of blood for twelve years. She spent all of her money trying to find the answer to her need. Nothing got better; everything grew worse. Then she heard of Jesus, and she saw something different. This woman, who had received a sentence of death twelve years earlier, didn't stop looking for the answer to her need. She continued saying, "I'm going to try to get better. At least I'm going to try." She refused to walk around talking about how bad it was. She refused to give up in hopelessness. She was out there grabbing at every-thing. Instead of having a pity party, she took control of the thing and tried to do something about it until faith arrived. She determined to look forward to her

God-given possibilities instead of backward to her yesterday's certainties.

And when faith finally got there, faith already had a platform on which to work in this woman because she had a never-die mentality and an open spirit to start with. When faith came, she just followed her faith.

That's how Elijah's servant responded, too. He said, "I'll keep going until I see what Elijah has seen, until I see the abundance of rain." The abundance of rain always moves you to action. You have to expect to see what you hear in the spirit.

Finally he could see. Verse 44 says, "Then it came to pass . . ." There is a time when it happens. Galatians 6:9 tells us, "And let us not grow weary while doing good, for in due season we shall reap if we do not lose heart."

God has perfect timing. God sees your work and labor of love that you've shown toward His name. By ministering to the saints, you stay in right relationship. Some people can't wait for God's perfect timing. They stop going to church, turn against their pastors and turn to the godless philosophies of man to find the answers they need.

> *The abundance of rain always moves you to action. You have to expect to see what you hear in the spirit.*

Elijah's servant didn't give up. Seven times he went back to take another look. Like the woman at Zarephath, he could have talked himself out of a miracle. But he didn't. Elijah was standing in the grace of God, but his servant couldn't access it.

Faith provides you access into the grace of God.

Romans 5:2 says, "Through [Jesus Christ] also we have access by faith into this grace in which we stand." Faith causes you to tap into the abundant resources of God.

Everything the devil tries to put on you has a time limit because Satan is a creature subject to time. But the things of God, the blessings that are not seen immediately, are eternal. His mercy extends to a thousand generations. His grace—and everything grace has appropriated—is available forever.

When we see and hear the abundance of rain, all we have to do is tell the devil that his time is up. That's what Elijah told the 450 prophets of Baal. Second Corinthians 4:17–18 says:

> For our light affliction, which is but for a moment [a limited span of time], is working for us a far more exceeding and eternal weight of glory, while we do not look at the things which are seen, but at the things which are not seen. For the things which are seen are temporary, but the things which are not seen are eternal.

Like Elijah, we have seen something different. We have seen a vision of the eternal abundance of rain. We're not afraid of the temporal things that cause us famine and thirst. We just need to tell the devil that his time is up. We can say, "The earth is the Lord's and the fullness therof. Sickness, get out of here. Poverty, loose your hold. Fear, you don't belong here any longer."

A Little Cloud

Finally, Elijah's servant came back with a different report. He said, "There arises a little cloud." That's how it happens; the abundance of rain begins rising up like a little cloud. Big moves start with little men. Big moves, great outpouring, mighty rivers start with just a drop of dew.

Great revelation comes from one *rhema* word from God in your spirit. And when it comes, you tap into another vein of understanding that is not available to the natural man. It comes from the Spirit. You will begin to live forward from this day on instead of looking backward to yesterday!

When it comes, you begin to see what others cannot see. You begin to hear what others cannot hear. And you can have what others cannot have. Elijah's servant said, "Behold, a cloud as small as a man's hand is coming up from the sea."

Often a move of God rises up looking like a man to start with. But before long the abundance of God beings to flow out of it. It may look like the voice of just one individual crying out. But before long, it sounds like the voice of many waters.

> *Great revelation comes from one* rhema *word from God in your spirit.*

It may begin with just one small rock being rolled away from the tomb. But before long you see the Rock of Ages, the Foundation Stone of all creation.

God always has a rain cloud that looks like a man's hand. It may be in the voice of a man or woman of God who hears what God is hearing, sees what God sees and says what God says.

You can be that cloud in your own family. Your church can be that cloud in your community. It happens when we stop sitting down. We must arise like a little cloud out of the sea of humanity.

You have to get up for the rain to fall. Every move of

God, every miracle starts with a natural action. It starts with a man's action in obedience to God. Miracles start because somebody believed and acted on his or her faith.

Have you heard and seen the abundance of rain? Are you willing to give what you have to get what you see? Has your faith found access into the grace of God where you can see the abundance of rain? Arise, step out in faith, and get into God's abundance of rain for today, from this day on!

---

*Henry H. Halley, *Halley's Bible Handbook* (Grand Rapids, MI: Zondervan, 1959),197.

210

Chapter 14

The Best Day
of Your Life

I BELIEVE THE best day of your life is ahead of you. I
see a time when you are free from binding iniquities,
from unforgiveness, dissatisfaction and depression. I see
a day when you are free from bad choices, when you
speak with the voice of faith and the echoes disappear,
when you live happily in the living room of your life. I
see a day when you have overcome. But sometimes to
get to the best day of your life, you have to go through
the worst day of your life.

David's Worst Day

We have looked at David's life several times in this book,
and I want to do so again, because in 1 Samuel 30, we see
David in one of the worst possible days a man could have.

> Now it happened, when David and his men came
> to Ziklag, on the third day, that the Amalekites had
> invaded the South and Ziklag, attacked Ziklag and

burned it with fire, and had taken captive the women and those who there, from small to great; they did not kill anyone, but carried them away and went their way. So David and his men came to the city, and there it was, burned with fire; and their wives, their sons and their daughters had been taken captive. Then David and the people who were with him lifted up their voices and wept, until they had no more power to weep.

— 1 SAMUEL 30:1–4

I would call this an unwelcome, discouraging circumstance, wouldn't you? David had been fighting for the Lord, only to come home and find his very household taken captive and, for all he knew, dead. Imagine seeing your hometown burned. Your house nothing but a foundation in the dirt. Your belongings strewn here and there, and not a loved one in sight.

Sometimes to get to the best day of your life, you have to go through the worst day of your life.

Do you realize that the enemy will attack you whether you are working for the Lord faithfully or not? He doesn't care if you are sinning or if your life is on the road toward godly maturity. He wants to hand you the worst day of your life—all day, every day.

God did not say we would not have bad days, but that those bad days would not amount to anything. He did not say, "No weapon formed against you shall come against you." He said, "No weapon formed against you shall prosper" (Isa. 54:17).

That's what happened to David. The enemy's weapons

212

came against him, but as we shall see, David made some wise choices, and God caused those weapons not to prosper.

It's no wonder that David and his men broke down and cried like little children when they came upon the city of Ziklag. These mighty warriors, who would go on to acts of bravery unlike any the world had ever seen, were instantly crushed in spirit.

Have you ever wept until you literally could not weep any more? Weeping is a beautiful gift of God, given to cleanse us on the inside. But weeping does not always cleanse. Sometimes it binds us up again, depending on where we have placed our faith. Weeping can become self-focused and cause us to be more bitter than when the tears began.

That is what happened with David's men.

> And David's two wives, Ahinoam the Jezreelitess, and Abigail the widow of Nabal the Carmelite, had been taken captive. Now David was greatly distressed, for the people spoke of stoning him, because the soul of all the people was grieved, every man for his sons and his daughters. But David strengthened himself in the LORD his God.
>
> — 1 SAMUEL 30:5–6

Weeping separated the man of God whose character stood head and shoulders above the rest. While the men became bitter, David encouraged himself in the Lord.

Encourage Yourself in the Lord

What happens when you encounter the worst day of your life? Let weeping cleanse you, and don't become bitter. Let the tears remind you of the One who will be your deliverance. Don't listen to or become frightened by the people around you who may want to stone you. The key to moving from your worst day to your best day is to encourage yourself in the Lord, because sometimes nobody else will encourage you. If you can't rely on yourself to speak the promises of God, upon whom can you rely? Take these steps:

- Remind yourself of God's faithfulness in the past.
- Speak the Word of God over your life.
- Praise God for the future He has in store for you.
- Read the Bible to see God's deliverance time and again.
- Speak the things that are not as though they are.
- Encourage yourself!

But make sure you encourage yourself *in the Lord*. Don't encourage yourself in your bank account, your position at work, your upcoming vacation, your future plans or anything else that can change in a moment of time. Rather, encourage yourself in the One who does not change, whose arm is not short, whose hand is not weak—who knows you by name.

David would not let discouragement keep its hold on him. If you look back at 1 Samuel 22, you can see that for a season of time he lived in a cave with four hundred distressed, discontented, indebted men from Israel—the rebels of that society. Can you imagine sleeping shoulder to shoulder with men like that who were full of turmoil on the inside? We can only guess how discouraging the mood in that cave was. But David did not become like them. He had a fire on the inside of him that those four hundred men caught, and when they came out of the cave they were a great fighting army.

Those same men may have wanted to stone him at Ziklag. But I can assure you, though they let bitterness grab hold of them in that moment, they would become some of God's greatest men.

Pursue, Overtake, Recover All

> Then David said to Abiathar the priest, Ahimelech's son, "Please bring the ephod here to me." Abiathar brought the ephod to David. So David inquired of the LORD, saying, "Shall I pursue this troop? Shall I overtake them?"
>
> — 1 SAMUEL 30:7–8

I love the fact that David never tried to do things on his own. He knew that God called people to be part of a body. One of his psalms says, "God sets the lonely in families" (Ps. 68:6, NIV). He was talking about Holy Spirit, kingdom of God families where each person has an anointing and a function, just like Abiathar the priest. David did not try to pretend he had all the answers. He went to the proper man with the proper anointing and pursued an answer with him.

I exhort you to do the same. Don't try to live the Christian life on your own. If you do, you will fall, and no one will be there to pick you up. Get into a Holy Spirit church with men and women who know how to pray, to heal, to pray prayers of deliverance and to break

A good priest teaches people to pray. He knows he cannot do their praying for them.

the yoke of bondage. Go where people know their gifts in the kingdom and are not afraid to use them.

David had a priest, Abiathar, with whom he could inquire of the Lord. But notice that Abiathar did not do the praying for David. A good priest teaches people to pray. He knows that he cannot do their praying for them. As pastors, we must teach people to pray and should not act as if we were the only ones who prayed prayers that work.

> And He [the Lord] answered him, "Pursue, for you shall surely overtake them and without fail recover all."
>
> — 1 SAMUEL 30:8

David consulted God on a plan of recovery, and God gave him a word: pursue, overtake and recover all. I believe that those words are for you as you read this book. Now is the time for you to inquire of the Lord. Many times the answer will be, "Pursue, overtake, and recover all."

Now is the time to go after what the devil has taken from you—the years lost to discouragement, dissatisfaction, unforgiveness or whatever you deal with. Now is the time to engage actively the enemies of your family, your life and your calling. God is calling many believers to stop weeping, step out of anger and bitterness and start overtaking and recovering what has been lost.

There is another thing from which we can learn from David. As he pursued the Amalekites, the marauding band of robbers who terrorized the region, he came upon an Egyptian who had lost his strength and was lying in a field. Suddenly David, the man who had encouraged himself just moments ago, became the encourager yet again as he encouraged this young man.

> And they gave him a piece of a cake of figs and two clusters of raisins. So when he had eaten, his strength came back to him; for he had eaten no bread nor drunk water for three days and three nights.
>
> — 1 SAMUEL 30:12

When a person is on the verge of recovering all that has been lost, that person can become an encouragement to others. We see it happening with David. Here is David, the one prophesied to be king over Israel, now having lost his wives and children and living as an outcast in the land of the Philistines. But instead of passing right by the Egyptian in need in the field, he takes a moment to encourage that man. Little did he know that by acting correctly and making the right choices, his whole life would change within seventy-two hours. By the end of that time, he would become king of Israel, get his wives back and receive back forty years of plunder from the Amalekites. Talk about going from your worst day to your best day!

You too can leave your worst day behind, but as we have seen before, it takes making the right choices. You must weep but not become bitter. Encourage yourself. Stand with others in prayer. Inquire of the Lord. Pursue the enemy. And encourage others along the way. When you have done these things, God will set you up for a great victory.

> *When a person is on the verge of recovering all that has been lost, that person can become an encouragement to others.*

This passage of Scripture goes on to say that David saw the Amalekites "spread out over all the land, eating and drinking and dancing, because of all the great spoil which they had taken from the land of the Philistines and from the land of Judah" (v. 16). Can you imagine how it would feel to come over the crest of a hill and see your enemies dancing as your wives sat captive in their camp? Eating food prepared from your crops and live-stock? Drinking wine and reveling in the money they stole from your house?

If you are anything like David, you would become righteously angry—which is what it sometimes takes to move into our best day. We can become righteously angry at what the enemy has stolen and at how he is abusing our inheritance. We can set our jaws firm and refuse to go back to our burned-out old life until we first recover all that we lost.

> So David recovered all that the Amalekites had car-ried away, and David rescued his two wives. And nothing of theirs was lacking, either small or great, sons or daughters, spoil or anything which they had taken from them; David recovered all.
>
> — 1 SAMUEL 30:18–19

Are you ready to recover all? Are you living in the worst day of your life? Learn from David's example. Refuse to be discouraged, and rely on the Word of the Lord. It will take you swiftly to your best day.

Chapter 15

Path of an Answer

DO YOU WANT to live victoriously for the rest of your life? Then do as David did and realize that it's the Lord's day, and that the One who made it is living in you and you in Him. I personally refuse to live in defeat. Whenever my mind tells me that trouble is brewing, I refuse to let that thought control me. Instead I simply believe that it is the day the Lord has made—and I rejoice and am glad in it. Why not take the day the Lord has made rather than the one the devil has made?

We have taken this journey together so you can be set free to live beyond yesterday. I believe that for many of you, that process is well under way. I believe the principles in this book will change your life forever.

Blind Bartimaeus taught us much already, but let me leave you with a few more observations about what he did that will help you to take the steps out of yesterday and into today:

- Bartimaeus got in the path of an answer. Have you? Are you going to a Holy Spirit church that believes in prayer and healing? Have you surrounded yourself with godly people who emanate the presence of God? What path are you in?

- He responded at the earliest opportunity. Have you let one altar call after another go by without responding? Have you refused a godly person's offer to lay hands on you and pray for you? Is your heart resistant or ready?

- His praise created an atmosphere of miracles. Do you praise God during the day? Do you enter into praise at church? When something bad happens, do you let it rob you of praising words? Is His praise continually in your mouth?

- Bartimaeus didn't let his circumstances set his boundaries. Have you? Do you believe more in your reputation than in your revelation? Is your life defined by what you see and by what people tell you, or by what you know to be true from God's Word?

- He responded like he believed the answer was near. Do you go to God in faith? Are you a skeptic when you approach the throne of grace, or do you come with childlike faith?

- His eyes were blind, but his faith was not. Do you have eyes that see, but faith that is blind? Or is your faith alive and active?

- The crowd was crying out for religion; Bartimaeus for reality. What are you more concerned with: the appearance of right living, or your deep-down relationship with God?

- He could have gone for sympathy, but he went for deliverance. Do you hold on to problems and weaknesses so you can draw ungodly sympathy out of other people? Or do you release and overcome your problems?

Bartimaeus showed us that problem people are God's purpose. We should never misjudge the cry for help. Bartimaeus used what he had to get what he wanted. He couldn't use his hands or his feet to make a living, because he didn't have useful eyes. The only thing he had was a voice and a revelation. You too must use what you have to get what you want. When you do, Jesus will override all obstacles and opposition to give you an answer, no matter what your problem is.

Too many people have been listening to the wrong crowd. They've been listening to the devil. They've been listening to daytime talk shows. Now is your time to rise up against the tide of mediocrity and let your mind be renewed according to God's Word. As Paul wrote, "Let this mind be in you which was also in Christ Jesus"

> *You too must use what you have to get what you want.*

(Phil. 2:5). Let's pray together that today will spell the end of living in the basement of yesterday, and that you will take God's offer to begin fresh and new, on the path toward a glorious tomorrow.

> *Heavenly Father, I'm tired of living in the basement of my yesterdays. I ask Your forgiveness for allowing my circumstances to set my boundaries. Lord, unstop my ears so that I can hear the sound of the abundance of*

rain. Remove the blinders from my spiritual eyes so that I can see the abundance of rain. And then, Father, I can voice the abundance of rain in my life as I move up to the living room of my today. Thank You, Lord, for hearing me. In Jesus' name, amen.

OTHER BOOKS
BY WALTER HALLAM MINISTRIES

Family Under Construction

*What Is Prosperity, and
Does God Want You to Have It?*

Succeeding Beyond Your Ability

*Money: Five Biblical
Strategies for Financial Success*

Delivered From Iniquity

Delivered From Depression

A City Called Heaven (Spanish)

Born Again

God Is More Than Enough

Understanding Tongues

The Rapture

Don't Look Back

For more information please write:
WALTER HALLAM MINISTRIES
P. O. Box 58970
Houston, TX 77258-8970

Your Walk With God Can Be Even Deeper...

With *Charisma* magazine, you'll be informed and inspired by the features and stories about what the Holy Spirit is doing in the lives of believers today.

Each issue:
- Brings you exclusive world-wide reports to rejoice over.
- Keeps you informed on the latest news from a Christian perspective.
- Includes miracle-filled testimonies to build your faith.
- Gives you access to relevant teaching and exhortation from the most respected Christian leaders of our day.

Call 1-800-829-3346 for 3 FREE trial issues
Offer #AOACHB

If you like what you see, then pay the invoice of $22.97 (**saving over 51% off the cover price**) and receive 9 more issues (12 in all). Otherwise, write "cancel" on the invoice, return it, and owe nothing.

Experience the Power of Spirit-Led Living

Charisma Offer #AOACHB
P.O. Box 420234
Palm Coast, Florida 32142-0234
www.charismamag.com

You can experience more of God's grace & love!